No Business Like E-Business

The Spectacularly Simple Secrets Behind How You Can Create A Web Site And Make Money With It

Ravi Jayagopal

NBLEB.com

Your Free Bonuses

Free Bonuses with your purchase of this book:

- ClickBank Download Protector PHP Script from WebmasterInABox.net – a **$34.95** Value
- Paypal Download Protector PHP (TLG) Script from WebmasterInABox.net – a **$34.95** Value
- TypingAssistant Productivity Software – a **$47.00** Value
- $50 Discount Coupon (Mail-in Rebate) for WebmasterInABox.net Suite – a **$50** Value
- And more...

See the updated bonuses list and the details for downloading them, at `NBLEB.com/bonuses.php`

Copyright Information

First Edition

ISBN: 978-0-9794376-0-1

Published by NicheWordsPublishing.com

Acknowledgements

Ekalavya's Thumb

You may not have heard of Ekalavya.

Ekalavya, as remembered by ancient East-Indian mythology, was a poor boy from the jungle. His dream was to become the greatest archer in the world.

The only way to do that was to learn from Guru Drona, one of the great warriors of all times. Drona, who was the archery tutor of the royal family, of course wanted his favorite disciple, Prince Arjuna to become the greatest archer of all times.

When Drona refused to accept Ekalavya as his disciple, a disappointed-yet-undeterred Ekalavya went home, and went on to practice archery in front of a statue of Drona he built himself.

Years later, Drona and Arjuna ran into a young boy in the forest, who was such an amazing archer that he was able to pierce the smallest of pebbles from thousands of yards away with his arrows. Troubled by Arjuna's jealous anger over seeing someone so much better than he, Drona cunningly claimed Ekalavya's left thumb as his "Guru Dakshina" (fees) for having used his statue and learned from him "indirectly".

Ekalavya cut off his thumb without flinching, without a second thought - and handed it to Guru Drona, letting Arjuna regain the status of the greatest archer ever, while creating history for his sacrifice.

I, Ravi Jayagopal - am Ekalavya. And my Guru Drona is my father, R.N. Jayagopal – one of the greatest Indian film writers of all times.

My father has penned some of the most beautiful poems ever written – the most touching, most romantic and the most inspiring lyrics ever. What I am today is just a reflection of his values, his integrity, his loyalty, his kindness and his tremendous character.

I dedicate my writing to my involuntary guru, my father, who has no clue that I have been secretly learning from him since my birth – who doesn't know that I have his statue built in my mind.

Dad - just don't ask me for my thumb, alright?

- - -

I thank my mother, Lalita, for her tremendous inner-strength, her will, perseverance, and for always being there for me and my father.

I thank my wife Veena. I've never met anyone with her level of passion and commitment towards their work. Just by being the perfectionist that she is, she inspires me to go beyond the ordinary.

I thank the greatest man alive, a man I worship: my Father-in-Law, Rajan. There is none more compassionate, considerate and giving as him. With him, I share a relationship like no other; he has been more than a father to me, and I hope I have been like a son to him.

Finally, there are two people who make me tick. Everything I do in my life revolves around them. I dedicate my life to my two children, Rhea and Rohan. Where would I be without them? Nowhere! I live for them, and I'd die for them. They are the only reasons for my existence. My world starts and ends with them. My beautiful children, I will always be there for you till the day I am gone.

-x-

Table of Contents

1. Solve, Don't Sell

People don't buy **products** – they buy **solutions**. Your product has to offer a *solution* that solves an immediate, burning *problem* that your prospective customer has.

Everyone has problems. Some of them are big: health problems, money problems, career problems, relationship problems. Some are smaller (I call them the *How-to Problems*): how to create a web site, how to run a business, how to learn a new skill, how to make stuff, and how to fix stuff.

If you have read the works of some of the great marketers like Dan Kennedy or Jay Abraham, you would know that people don't buy something for the sake of buying – they buy something because they are hoping it will solve a "problem" or "need" or "want".

More often than not, this problem is a *burning* problem or *immediate* need - and people want solutions N.O.W. If you help them solve that need, they will not only open up their wallets, but they will also open up their minds and hearts (depending on how big a problem you are solving). This makes them not just an immediate customer, but a customer for life, willingly trying – and maybe even buying - any (relevant) products that you may try to sell them in the future.

I use the word "product" loosely in this book, to represent tangible, physical products, downloadable digital products, as well as online and off-line services. I also refer to one who sells a product or service as a "merchant".

The 2nd School of Marketing

Market the Sizzle, Not the Steak

Another breed of products is where you sell an experience. You are not solving a problem for anyone, but instead selling a dream – the sizzle – targeting people's wants, not needs.

Do you think people would spend $370,000[1] for a car if car makers just tried to fulfill a *need* (which is to be able to get from one place to another?)

Do you become richer or better looking or more successful simply by driving one of these cars? Or would you be less prone to accidents just because the alloy wheels cost about $25,000 each?

Nope, accidents happen to everyone – not just to the middle class, not just to the poor, and not just to drivers of the "cheap" cars.

So what is it about a car that makes people shell out that kind of big bucks? Well, it's the *experience* that car makers sell.

No, it's not about safety, mileage, or reliability.

It's about that rush you get when you floor the pedal and zoom away on the highway, hugging the curves of the hills, (conveniently, as the ads will show, with no other vehicles – or cops - within a 20 mile radius) with the top down, the wind in your face (or the hair of your significant other).

---

[1] Yes, that is the price of a real car, the Pagani Zonda, a 200-mph Italian racer built in Italy and powered by a Mercedes-Benz AMG V-12.

People have needs – and then they have wants. All you gotta do is pick one, and fulfill it.

Great Marketing, Mediocre Products

I'm sure you have heard of **Buyer's Remorse,** the extreme feeling of paranoia, guilt or uncertainty that occurs after you have bought something rather impulsively. Actually, people often feel buyer's remorse even when they've done a fair amount of research and the purchase is a planned event.

There are shopping addicts who end up talking themselves out of this remorse – and then there are those who go through with the purchase, but end up returning the product and requesting a refund.

Buyer's remorse is among the biggest challenges to you as a seller. You could be the greatest sales copy writer, the coolest web site designer, the savviest Internet marketer – but there is a limit as to how long you can trick people into buying a mediocre product with your excellent sales page.

If your product doesn't completely solve someone's problem, your buyers will be lining up for that refund faster than those orders rolled in.

Buyer's Remorse

Stephen Pierce, a marketer who suddenly appeared out of nowhere and shot to fame (and money) within a very short period of time in 2002, raises some powerful questions about the proverbial buyer's remorse in one of his presentations called "Moolah Map".

When was the last time someone with a splitting headache, purchased a bottle of migraine pills at the pharmacy, got cured of the headache, went back to the pharmacy and asked for a refund because they had buyer's remorse? Or because they felt they weren't sure if it was the *right product* for them? Or because they weren't sure if they *paid too much for it*?

If your product delivers what it promises, then you have practically eliminated buyer's remorse. When you solve an immediate need and your customer sees the results that you promised, they will neither ask for a refund, nor will they hesitate from gladly recommending you to anyone who they think might have a similar problem or need.

Differentiate or Die

Even if you deliver what you promise, it still doesn't mean someone will buy your product.

Selling a product is a two-step process:

- Creating a remarkable product
- Getting people to buy (which usually involves switching from using your competitor's product)

Unless you give people a real reason to switch, it doesn't matter how "awesome" or "cool" or "cheap" or "must have" your product is – people simply won't buy it (figuratively, and literally).

For most people, switching from one product to another presents a hassle. It is a hassle to switch your direct deposit (you've got that form to fill and fax), a hassle to re-create all those online bill payments you've already scheduled, a hassle to re-train your partner, spouse, child, or employee to use a new product, a hassle to ask your purchasing department to create a new vendor in the database, a hassle to convince your buyer to buy a new product that does pretty much the same as the old one, heck, it is a hassle even to switch to a new bath soap or toothpaste!

Switching also represents challenging the status quo, doing something new, something different, which also involves failure. You've just recommended this new product - what if it doesn't work the way it is supposed to? What if it breaks too soon? What if the customer service or technical support sucks? What if it ends up wasting everyone's time? It is your name and reputation on the line. Will your spouse/partner/ employees criticize you for it? Will your boss hold you responsible? Will your productivity go down because of this? Will it become too much of a head ache to manage?

This is why you have to differentiate. You've got to give people a compelling reason to buy your product, or switch from your competitor's product. You cannot do this just with slick marketing and Super Bowl ads.

If you have noticed, some of the world's most successful products are among the least marketed. When was the last time you had to convince someone to use Windows instead of Linux for their desktop? How many Volkswagen or Mercedes ads do you see on TV? How many Macintosh PowerBook owners have you heard complaining about their laptop? How often do you hear complaints that Japanese cars suck?

On the flipside, if your product is not perfect, but still solves your customer's problem, you could end up laughing your way to the bank. Case in point: Microsoft.

Everybody complains about how unstable Microsoft operating systems are – but it is such a colossal challenge to come up with something as usable and widely integrated as Microsoft's products.

Being a hardcore techie myself, I still don't own a Linux desktop. Sure, all my web sites are hosted on Linux, and I do almost all of my programming on Linux machines – but my *primary* desktop – the one that has all of my tools that I use for my e-Business - like email , office automation , printing, faxing - are all still Windows™ -based.

I use Windows XP pro on my laptop, use Eudora for email, Microsoft Office for all my office documentation, DreamWeaver for web site development, Eclipse for Java development, Camtasia Studio for my flash-video needs, and so on. I would actually be completely lost without Windows, because most of the tools I use are not available for other operating systems.

When you have a remarkable product, you won't have anyone wanting to return it. So, don't waste time on improving your "returns" process – focus on eliminating the need for refunds altogether.

Some call it creating your "USP" (Unique Selling Proposition). Scott T. Gross calls it "Positively Outrageous Service". I call it "Fanatic'nical Support". Seth Godin calls it the "Purple Cow". Sheldon Bowles and Ken Blanchard call it "Raving Fans".

Doesn't matter what you call it. Differentiate – or Die.

2. How to Make Money Online

So you are betting people will pay you money - people who have no idea who you are, where you are from, or whether or not you are even a real person.

You are hoping they will use their credit card on your web site, in the middle of the night, from the remotest corner in the world, to buy whatever it is that you are selling.

This "product" that you are selling on your web site is the entire foundation of your e-Business. How much you sell, and how successful you will be in the long run, is dominated to a substantial extent by your product. Of course, there are many other factors too, but your product is all where it starts.

- How well you can sell depends on many of the following aspects of your product:
- How big is the problem you are solving? People will pay more if you can solve larger issues (investments, cure a disease or ailment, make more money). They will pay less if your product can solve smaller problems (how to garden, how to fix a leaking toilet.)

- Is it for mass consumption (toothpaste, stationery, toilet paper) or a specialized product (software for hospitals or automobiles)?
- How large is your target market? Is it for mass consumption, or only for those who match certain demographics?
- How good is your product? Is it good enough, great, or absolutely remarkable?
- How much of your target market are you able to reach? How often, and how effectively? Are they geeks and nerds? Or moms and pops? Are they kids?
- How much of an expert does your target market consider you, if at all?
- How well implemented is your overall marketing strategy (viral marketing, affiliate programs, search engine optimization, joint ventures, newsletters, Pay-Per-Click and Pay-Per-Action revenue)?
- How powerful is your marketing copy? Does your site communicate in a professional, yet informal way? Is your copy naturally "cool"? Does it have a personality? Does it exude your (or your organization's) personality?
- How big is your email list?
- How different are you from your competition?
- How trustworthy are you?
- How easily can your visitors and customers recommend you to others?
- How many repeat-customers do you get?
- How thrilled are your customers with your product and customer service and support?
- Are you providing your customers with great service at every single touch-point of your e-business?

Your marketing doesn't have to always be the biggest piece of your plan. But your product certainly does.

Heard of the saying "don't judge a book by its covers"?

It is like that brilliant but weird employee at work, who is not the most "normal" person, and definitely not the friendliest one. But people will tolerate all of that employee's quirks, weird behavior and mood swings, if that person is really good at what she does, because nothing negatively impacts a company's bottom-line more than pretty-looking, smooth talkers who neither have much *upstairs,* nor can get the job done.

I can't remember the number of times I have been told something to the effect of "go check out this (insert business name here – like "restaurant"), their service is not the greatest, but the (insert product name here: like "food") is really awesome".

I'm sure you have been referred to other people, products or services in a similar way, where the exterior did not appear to be great, but the actual product or service itself was so good that people still recommended them to you.

Many years ago, when my daughter was an infant, her pediatrician was a rude, short-tempered, obnoxious guy – but he had such a golden touch with his patients, that I – along with countless other parents – was able to tolerate him, because the way he (literally) treated my daughter (his patient), because I thought this was more important than how he treated me (as a person).

The end result was that this guy was constantly overbooked, and the parents, along with their sick children, poured into his office in hordes to have their children treated by him.

This is why historically, some of the most successful low budget movies with completely unknown faces, have gotten off to a slow start at the box office – and as people saw them and found out how good it was, ticket sales went through the roof in the subsequent weeks as word spread. ("Hey, this <unadvertised> movie that you probably haven't heard of has no stars – but it has some amazing actors and a brilliant plot").

On the contrary, we sometimes buy stuff mainly because of its cover, but more about that later.

Nuts, Bolts, Nails and Screws

We shall be delving into all the pieces of creating a web site and making money online, in as much detail as is relevant here, without having to write a separate book about each topic.

Here's a quick overview of what's coming up:

- What to Sell Online (and How To Sell It)
- Registering a Domain Name and Web Hosting
- Planning Your Web Site, Design & Programming
- Building Quality Content
- Making Money With Google Adsense
- Traffic Generation
- Search Engine Optimization (SEO)
- Credit Card Processing
- Mailing List Creation and Management
- Internet Marketing
- Converting Visitors Into Customers
- Referral and Affiliate Marketing
- Productivity, Tricks, Hacks and Time Management

3. What to Sell Online?

People come up to me all the time and ask, "How can I make money online?"

To me, that is like asking how many stars there are in the sky – because that really is the number of ways you can make money online. But the problem is that most folks get lost trying to cut through the clutter of information online and in figuring out what really works.

To put it in a way-too-small nutshell, here are 4 ways in which you can make money online:

1. Selling *advertisements* on your web site

2. Selling *other* people's products *without* a web site

3. Selling *other* people's products *with* your web site

4. Selling *your* own products *with* your web site.

Note: When I say 'products', I mean 'services' too.

In this chapter, we'll explore the various ways to generate revenue from your web site.

Selling Advertisements on Your Web Site

There are 3 types of ads – Cost-Per-Impresssion, Pay-Per-Action (PPA) and Pay-Per-Click (PPC).

Cost-Per-Impression (CPM)

An "impression" is nothing but a "Page View" – which means, one page being viewed once by a visitor. So, when someone arrives at your web site and sees your home page, it is counted as "1 impression". If they stay on and visit 9 more pages on your site, your site has generated a total of 10 impressions.

CPM - which is actually **C**ost **P**er thousand i**M**pressions - is where an advertiser pays you just to display ads on your web site, and you get paid "Per Impression" (every time the ad is displayed on your web site). Advertisers usually purchase impressions by the "thousands".

So, if an advertiser pays a CPM of $1, it means that for every thousand times their advertisement (text or banner) is displayed on your web site, you get paid $1. So, if your web site generated 50,000 impressions (page views), then the advertiser pays you:

50 (thousand impressions) x $1 (per thousand) = $50.

If you displayed 4 CPM ads on the same page, then you get paid $200 ($50 x 4).

If your traffic improved from 50,000 impressions to 500,000 impressions, then you stand to make $2000 ($200 x 10).

While the math looks very impressive, in reality, these stats and revenue do not apply to the average site. CPM ads do not convert into paying customers very well (when was the last time you clicked on a big banner on Yahoo and purchased something?). This is why they are not widely available to all sites.

While this kind of advertising is an excellent vehicle for "branding" (for creating consumer "awareness" about a product), they are not particularly profitable for most advertisers. Just displaying an ad on your site doesn't really do the advertiser much good - the advertiser makes money only when someone clicks on their ad, goes on to their web site, and finally takes some action (like purchasing their product(s) or even signing up for the advertiser's newsletter).

So, it is rare these days to come across CPM deals from advertisers. And even if you did find an offer, you will find that the payout for the average site is very minimal – anywhere from $0.01 (yes, 1 cent) to maybe $1.00 CPM.

The sites which get the larger CPM deals are the big guns – like Yahoo, CNN, MSNBC – which get tens of millions of page views and millions of visitors every day.

CPM mainly works when the goal is just to improve branding. The more times people see your name and logo and your message, the more likely they are to associate your product with a particular niche when it's time for them to buy.

CPM is not a realistic source of revenue for your site, at least not to start with. So, let's look at the next model.

Cost-Per-Action (CPA)

This is a very popular model of revenue generation. In this model, the advertiser pays you a bounty (commission) if the visitor you sent them takes some form of action.

This action could be one of two things:

Your referral (visitor) signs up for something on the advertiser's web site – i.e., a newsletter, a form requesting more information, or some kind of a permission list, where the advertiser is allowed to contact the referral by email, snail-mail or phone (depending on what information the sign-up form requests) to send them ads or some specific information. This is also commonly known as lead generation (or Pay-Per-Lead).

Your referral goes on to purchase something from the advertiser. This is also known as Affiliate Marketing. You are the "affiliate" (a.k.a associate or partner) of the advertiser (in this case, the seller). The seller pays you a "commission" – which is a flat fee or a portion of the profits – for every visitor you send to the seller's site who ends up purchasing some product from the seller's web site. Affiliate Marketing is explained in greater detail in a later chapter.

Pay-Per-Click (PPC)

This is probably the fastest and easiest way to start making money online. In this model, you get paid when someone "clicks" on an advertisement on your web site.

The most popular PPC service provider is Google's Adsense ™. Adsense is my #1 recommendation for PPC ad revenue (versus dealing with ad agencies) which serves up content-related ads on your site, and pays you per click. The actual earnings *per click* is minimal by itself (we'll see how to increase this later), but increasing the volume of these clicks can quickly add up to big dollars if your site gets thousands of visitors and hundreds (or even tens of thousands) of page views.

There are other similar PPC providers like Yahoo Publisher Network, Bidvertiser.com, Text-Link-Ads.com and AdBrite.com. But from my experience, Adsense converts the best, and also makes the most revenue for most publishers. These results can vary from web site to web site, and your results may be completely different than mine. The only real way to verify this is by testing different revenue options and tracking the results for your self.

Once you sign up for a Google Adsense account (you have to be approved first), you can log in to your account online and get some text (JavaScript code) that you insert in your web pages where you want the ads to show up. When someone visits that page on your site, based on various factors like the page title, your web site's domain name, page name and content, Google figures out the best "relevant" ads to show, and displays them on the page in real time.

For example, if you have a web site about baby names, your visitor will see ads related to babies, mothers, pregnancy, parenting, etc.

Someone clicks on your ads, and you make money! Easy money, right? *Yes*, and *No*. While it sounds very simple to be able to throw up some ads on your site and make money each time someone clicks on them, there are a number of challenges with PPC.

It is easy to make your first few cents (or even a dollar) as soon as your advertisements start showing up on your site. However, without traffic, that's where your revenue will remain – at just a few cents – which is no good when it comes to paying even your web hosting bill, let alone making a living online!

If you are wondering about clicking on your own ads, or having friends and relatives click on your ads, don't even think about it! When (not *if*) the service provider figures out the fraud, they can seize your funds, terminate your account, and even ban you from getting another account ever again.

Pay-per-click fraud happens in millions of dollars, and providers like Google and Yahoo have large teams of people dedicated to just tracking, monitoring and policing potentially fraudulent clicks. Therefore, if you try to artificially inflate clicks and boost your earnings in a fraudulent way, you will lose your account and your earnings very, very fast. Don't even consider this as an option!

To make a lot of money with PPC, you need a lot of traffic. The more visitors your web site has, the more pages they will (may) visit, and the more ads they will (may) click on. Of course, these are only possibilities, not a given formula, but by driving a lot of traffic to your site, you increase the probability of them visiting more pages, which in turn leads to an increase in the probability of people clicking on your ads.

More Traffic + More Pageviews = More Clicks

The formula is oversimplified, but you get the idea.

You can find out more about PPC revenue in the chapter "How to Earn a Nice Little Paycheck From Google".

The bottom-line for PPC revenue is that you won't make a large amount of money unless you have a web site that is generating hundreds of thousands of page views and getting at least a couple of hundred thousand visitors a month.

One way to increase your PPC revenue is to target a topic which will trigger higher paying ads. For example, the ads on a site about insurance or consolidating credit card loans will pay you more than, for example, ads on a site about basket weaving. It is sheer common sense – the more money there is to be made in a market (*loans* vs. *basket weaving*), the more advertisers will be willing to pay Google for their ads. This translates into earning more from your Adsense clicks.

But keep in mind, that not all advertisers opt to advertise on third-party web sites. As an "AdWords" advertiser (the flip side of the "Adsense" coin), you can opt out of advertising on web sites other than Google, and choose to display your ads only on Google properties (like search engine results pages, Gmail, etc).

Even if you see or hear about high paying keywords, it is not necessary that those same prices will be passed on to you as a publisher. The high prices per click are what the advertisers pay Google, but Google only passes on a small percentage of those per-click cents to you. So, it is not a firm rule that you will always get the same percentage of the actual cost per click from Google. Google goes to great lengths to avoid disclosing this formula, which is not a bad thing, because the more people know about the inner workings of such services, the more these services can be gamed and spammed, thus rendering them useless, or increasing the costs for everyone involved.

The more targeted the audience, the higher rates you will be able to charge for displaying ads on your web site, and the more clicks you will get from your PPC ads.

With targeted traffic, even if the volume is low, you will still make decent money. But remember that without heavy traffic, it will never be enough to quit your day job.

If you want ad revenue to be your primary source of income from your web site, then you will have to have a substantially large site with lots of content that has what your target audience wants – or needs.

Now don't start thinking about becoming the next Yahoo! I strongly recommend against this model because you just can't win with the existing giants like Yahoo, MSN and Google (even if you were at the top of the Internet game).

You are better off creating a "niche site" or "vertical site" with content and products laser-focused towards your target market.

Niche sites specialize in a particular product, category, or consumer segment. Here, you will need to focus all your time, money and effort towards creating a web site that will bring in highly targeted visitors who are looking for products or services or even just plain information, in your area of expertise.

For instance, you could create a niche site about real estate. You would have all the following content areas on your site:

- Articles with tips for first time home buyers
- What to watch out for when buying a home
- Tips for those refinancing
- Articles on how to search for real estate
- On whether to use a realtor or do it yourself
- How to go pick a realtor
- How to sell it on your own
- You could also branch out a little along the same lines, and have:
- Home improvement tips
- Recommendations for repair tools
- How-to articles, manuals, ebooks, guides, tutorials
- Ask-an-expert sections
- Forums to exchange information with other visitors
- Your target audience in this case is:
- Home buyers in general (and importantly first time buyers)
- Looking to buy a second home or vacation home

- Looking to refinance or get a home equity loan
- Want to learn about home improvement
- Looking for information about decorating and home upgrades

Your potential sponsors are:

- Google Adsense and other PPC providers
- Mortgage brokers and lenders like Banks and other financial institutions who will pay you hefty sums if you can provide them with qualified leads who are looking to finance a new home or simply re-finance or get a home equity line of credit.
- Realty services – both online (Realtor.com) and offline
- Realtors themselves
- Sellers who are in the market to sell their home or other property
- Large home improvement product vendors – like Home Depot or Lowe's
- Companies that manufacture products for the home and home owner
- At-home service providers that do plumbing, landscaping, fencing, kitchen remodeling, roofing, painting, lawn mowing, maid services, etc.

A really good example of a niche site is `BobVila.com`. Bob Vila is generally considered an expert in home improvement. His web site is focused on home improvement.

But how did I get to know about him? It was when he was a celebrity guest on one of my all-time favorite shows on TV, Tim Allen's "Home Improvement". Do you think the creators of the show randomly picked him to appear on this show?

Ever since I saw that show, I have associated Bob Vila with Home Improvement. And when I first bought a house and wanted to research the best way to paint walls, guess which was the first web site I visited? BobVila.com, of course!

When it comes to ad revenue for small web sites, there are basically two eras:

* Pre-Adsense

* Post-Adsense

Pre-Adsense Era

Generating ad revenue from your site before AdSense, was a tough "sell" – both literally and figuratively – especially for the small guy. Selling ads yourself was one of the hardest parts.

You first had to have a reasonably popular, commercial, mainstream site with a huge number of page views, to even be considered for review by the hotshot Internet-based ad agencies. One of my own sites (BabyNamesIndia.com) was getting over 300,000 page views a month in 2000, but I still couldn't get any of the mainstream ad agencies to buy my ads.

Finding individual and corporate sponsors directly was an even bigger deal - you had to have the right contacts, you had to have a reasonable reputation online, you had to find and hang-out at online communities where potential sponsors frequently visited, you had to join co-ops, do joint ventures, and all sorts of monkeying around even to scrape a few dollars in ad revenue.

If you were not a big name or didn't have a big site, then you were practically finished even before you started.

And then came Adsense.

Post-Adsense Era

Life is much easier for small e-Business owners like you and me ever since AdSense welcomed publishers to paste some code on their web site, have Google Ads show up that matched the content on the actual page on which it showed up, and get a small share of the profits if your visitors clicked on those ads.

Now, this is not guaranteed revenue, like CPM (Cost per 1000 impressions) ads where the sponsor pays you a fixed fee for every 1000 times their ad is viewed by viewers on your site.

However, because Google uses a very smart technology that displays ads based on the contents of your web site, users are more likely to click on these ads, and your chances of earnings just skyrocketed.

As mentioned before, the key to generating substantial ad revenue from Google Adsense is traffic. The more traffic you get, the more clicks you will get, and in turn, will earn that much more money from Google.

Traffic will come if you have great content, and if you do the right things to make sure that people can find you. There are a lot of things you can do to increase traffic, as we will see in later chapters, but the foundation of a great web site which attracts huge numbers of people, is lots of great content.

"Content, content, content". Yes, Content is King, especially if you want to make money from selling advertisements.

Niche Sites

You will need to create a web site, with lots of content, which will bring you lots of page views, which will get you lots of clicks, which will eventually make you lots of money from ad revenue.

Lots of content means plenty of articles, tutorials, how-to guides, user forums, and providing your users with ways to create and share content – all focused at a highly targeted audience.

These types of targeted web sites are called "Niche Sites" in web lingo. Niche sites, when correctly executed, generate huge amounts of traffic and create loyal users who create a lot of content themselves, refer others to your site, and bring in even more traffic.

With some work, you could create a snowball effect, whereby users are bringing in more users who are creating even more content which in turn brings more users!

And thanks to open-source software, you can do all of this without having any site designing or web programming skills. For creating niche sites, the software I recommend is Mambo Content Management System, at Mamboserver.com

Blogs

You can also generate money from even more focused content called Blogs (we**blogs**).

Blogging is the art of being able to publish at the speed of thought. Think of it as an archive of your opinions, outlook and your thoughts, that you share with your site visitors.

Blog software allows you to do this without having to worry about HTML, coding, maintaining an index of your posts, organizing, and sorting. The software does everything except create the content.

That's where you come in, and provide meaningful, relevant and useful insights about your area of expertise – a commentary relevant to your target audience.

Every blog must have a reason to exist - it could be just about keeping your friends updated about your life, or it could be as serious as blogging to create your individual brand or it could be about getting people to vote for you.

Regardless of the intention behind it, blogs have become an extremely powerful medium to quickly spread your message, thoughts and ideas.

Google put blogs on the international map when they bought Blogger.com, the already popular free blogging service. Blogs played a big part in raising funds and spreading the message and brand and "tech-coolness factor" of the candidates during the 2004 US Presidential election.

Blogs have been published about what blogs are, how to publish blogs, and even how to make money from blogs.

There are both free- and paid- services available that host everything for you, and then there's both free and paid software, which you install on your web site. Here's a small list of what's available out there:

Hosted Services

Blogger.com (Free): Google's service is among the most popular free, hosted services.

Wordpress.com (Free): This is a free, hosted version of the most popular, open-source blogging application, WordPress. You can also download the blog application from WordPress.org and install it on your own site.

TypePad.com (Paid): This is among the more popular, commercial hosted services that charge a monthly fee.

Installed software

WordPress.org (Free): This is what powers my own blog at `RavisRants.com` and the free online service, `WordPress.com`.

Joomla.com (Free) - Very powerful CMS (Content Management System), that powers one of my own niche sites.

Some of My Favorite Blogs/Newsletters:

* **Monday Morning Memo** at `Wizardacademy.com/showmemo.asp`

* **Seth Godin's Blog** at `sethgodin.typepad.com`: One of the most powerful business blogs, Seth's uncanny street-smart marketing sense tells you all about purple cows and lying marketers.

* **LifeHacker.com** – A blog that relentlessly provides fresh content about tools and technology, updated multiple times a day.

* **Gizmodo.com/Engadget.com** - The ultimate blogs for the person who loves to hang out at places like Radio Shack and Best Buy (isn't that every man alive?)

Check out the Google Adsense ads on some of these blogs. These blogs get huge traffic because of their great content, and traffic ultimately converts to ad revenue.

Let's say (hypothetically speaking) that for every 1000 page-views (a page-view is one page viewed by a visitor), you make roughly about $1 in Adsense revenue. So for 10,000 page views per day, you will make about $10 per day, which converts to (roughly) about $300 per month.

Based on this rather simplified formula, the way to increase your revenue would be to increase your page-views, which can happen in two ways – create more pages worth visiting, and bring more visitors to visit those pages.

If you could generate 50,000 page views a day, your income would shoot up to $50 a day - or $1500 per month.

Then if you move on to creating more niche sites with more pages on a different topic, and if you could create 10 such web sites each bringing in about $15,000 a day, you now have a revenue stream of $15,000 per month!.

That is how scalable the online revenue model is. You do the work once, and it pays off for a long time to come. (Of course, you still need to maintain and update your sites often).

So, you could create a blog about a highly focused topic, and serve ads on this site. However, if your blog is about trying to build your brand and eventually increasing sales for your product, displaying ads and sending your visitors away to your competitors does not make much sense. So make sure your revenue strategy is consistent with your goals for your web site.

Selling Other People's Products Without a Web Site

To understand this, you need to know how Affiliate Programs work.

In PPC marketing, like we saw earlier, a web site owner is willing to pay a PPC service (like Adsense) anywhere from a few cents to many dollars for each click (generated by the service) that sends a visitor to his site.

The advertiser (site owner) creates ads, and then sets his own price per click that the advertisement gets.

These ads are shown by say, Adsense, on the search results pages on Google, and optionally on the web sites of the millions of other web site owners who have content that is relevant to your ad.

One of the marketing segments spawned by Pay-per-click advertising services like Google's Adsense, is that you can now combine it with "Affiliate Marketing" and redirect the visitor who just clicked on your ad, directly to your affiliate link for a product that you are promoting.

In this model, it is possible that you may be competing with the actual seller themselves (the merchant), which creates a conflict of interest (though this conflict really works to the advantage of the merchant – let the affiliate bear the burden of the clicks, weed out the tire-kickers, and pay only for a successful sale.)

Also, Google is very strict about not allowing multiple affiliates competing with each other to send traffic to more or less the same site.

The last time I checked, Google allows only one affiliate link per keyword combination. So, if another affiliate is already advertising for a given keyword, then your ad that redirects the visitor to the same merchant will be rejected.

Even if Google doesn't allow it, there are still other PPC providers that still let you do this. So, not all is lost.

But this model is mentioned mainly for your information, and is not recommended, especially when you are just getting started.

Selling Other People's Products on Your Web Site

This is where you are an affiliate and promote other people's products on your web site using special links, in return for a share in the revenue. See the chapter on "Affiliate Marketing" for details.

Selling Your Products on Your Web Site

This is probably the most profitable way to make money online. When you have your own product, you have the most leverage on how to sell it, how to price it, and what promotions and offers to make to potential buyers.

Heck, you could even *give away* some of your products for free as a bonus for purchasing your other products. When you own the product, there isn't anyone to question how much you sell it for, or how you promote that product.

The biggest profits lie in owning the product, because the biggest piece of the pie always goes to the one who has created or owns the product - at least in the digital-product world).

However, when you are an affiliate promoting somebody else's products, you are sending hard-earned traffic to somebody else's web site (the merchant who is actually selling the product). So, the merchant is the one who gets the traffic, the page views, the newsletter sign-ups, and most importantly, controls the conversion rate.

If you send the merchant a thousand visitors, and not one of them purchased the product, then the merchant obviously has a lousy conversion rate – and you have just wasted all of your efforts in promoting a loser. However, if it were your own product, *you* control the traffic, the marketing copy, the site layout, and most importantly, you have the most influence over the conversion rate. If something is not working, you can change it. You can tweak, test, experiment with your sales copy, your offer, your pricing, and just about anything, to see what gets you the highest conversions.

And you will also be the one building that all-important mailing list of prospects, newsletter subscribers, and customers. In online marketing, the money is in the list. Yes, it's worth repeating again – "The Money Is In the List!"

If you have newsletter subscribers, you can influence them to become prospects.

If you have a list of prospects, you can follow up with them and convert them into buying customers.

If you have a list of customers, you can follow up with them and sell them more through back-end sales.

The list of what you can do with a "list" is never ending - the opportunities are endless.

For some of the highly popular digital products online, "Super Affiliates" (site owners with the biggest mailing lists with a highly targeted subscriber list) earn as much, or sometimes even more, then the owner of the product. This is similar to the real world scenario, where the Wal-marts and the K-marts (retailers) who make more money on the sale of a product, than the manufacturer themselves.

In the offline world, retail is where the most money is. However in the online world, the biggest piece belongs to the product owners and the "Super Affiliates" - the big dogs of marketing, who own huge lists and promote these products to thousands of people on their email list.

When you own the product, you have the power to make deals with other site owners and affiliates, including how much commission to pay them per sale, and engage these affiliates to promote your product in return for a piece of the profits.

You can make different kinds of deals with different types of affiliates, site owners, and even offer package deals to sell as a part of other people's products.

And finally, *you* will be the one building the list. Even if your visitors don't buy your product right away, you can still collect their contact information, add them to an autoresponder (automated series of pre-written emails) and convert them into customers over time.

But all of this freedom, flexibility and power come at a price – it is your responsibility to create a great product, with a great direct-marketing web site that has powerful sales copy to persuade the highest possible percentage of visitors into buying your product. In addition, you also have the responsibility of shipping and handling, pre-sales enquiries, post-sales customer service, technical support, refunds, etc.

There are some tools available which can help you automate a lot of these back-office tasks, but these come at a price too.

Therefore, the more profits you want, the more risk you need to take, and the more work you need to do. But as the saying goes, the best things in life come at a price ;-)

Your product does not even have to be an actual "product".

Your product is technically anything that brings you revenue – whether that revenue is generated through an instant purchase of your product, or something that eventually leads to a purchase.

It could be an actual product you sell, it could be someone else's product that you are selling, it could be access to content that you have created; or you could simply be selling advertisements on the content that you have created, using an advertisement service like Google's Adwords program at `Google.com/adwords`.

The most important part of your e-Business is figuring out the revenue model. If you can understand the need for your e-business to make a profit, you already know more than all those dot.com executives who raised millions of dollars in venture capital, based on a "cool idea" that made absolutely no business sense. Many of them did not even have a half-decent product, but were spending millions of dollars on SuperBowl commercials.

Selling your own product is such an important topic, that I have devoted an entire chapter for that. So keep reading.

4. Selling Your Own Products

The highest profits in an offline business is often made not by the manufacturer, but by the retailer – especially giants like Wal-mart or Sears – who are willing to invest thousands of dollars in your product and buy in the hundreds of thousands for all of the stores in their chain - and for the very same reason, can dictate margins to such an extent, that you have very little option but squeeze out your profits.

Remember, a Wal-mart has many options when it comes to buying a hair dryer or toothpaste or a microwave oven. But there is only one Wal-mart or Sears who can send your sales through the roof overnight.

However, because the Internet is such a direct-seller's dream medium, those who are selling their own products online, are the ones who get to keep the biggest chunk of the profits.

Even giants like Amazon, who spend millions of dollars on warehousing and merchandising, are able to still make a profit because the entire world is their marketplace when it comes to the Internet. They are not restricted in their reach because anyone anywhere in the world who has a computer and an Internet connection – and a credit card, of course – is a potential customer.

Digital or Physical?

Once you decide to sell your own physical products, unless you already own or manufacture a product, you have the option of selling a physical "tangible" product that needs to be shipped – or you could sell a digital product – like an eBook (electronic book), a collection of files (audio or video or text), or even plain information in the form of downloadable reports, subscription services or pay-per-access services.

Advantages of Physical Products

Nothing beats snuggling into bed with a good book – or relaxing on the couch with the morning newspaper, with a hot cup of coffee and a warm, toasted bagel with cream cheese, on a lazy Sunday morning. Nope, the computer monitor doesn't come even close.

Nothing tempts like the tabloids at the superstore checkout counter. Or the smell of freshly baked croissants in the bakery section (especially if you made the mistake of shopping on an empty stomach). Or the deliciously crisp image quality of a 60" plasma TV. Or the mind-blowing sounds emanating from a wee-sized Bose home theatre audio system.

We are physical creatures. Many times, it is hard for us humans to understand "meta-physical" concepts – concepts that are not "concrete" – ideas that cannot be given a physical "shaped" in our minds – thoughts that are not "tangible".

Physical products have an air of "authenticity" about them that digital products can only dream of.

An author of an actual book that is sold on Amazon.com somehow seems to command more respect than an "ebook" writer whose ebook is sold only on his own site.

Someone who manufactures $99-value software shipped on CD appears more authentic than someone selling a "downloadable" software program that has no "visual" image to display.

That is why, most digital products, even though they have no physical, visual image in the real world, are often depicted on sales pages using an actual image that either resembles an actual book (for e-books), a magazine (for reports) or software boxes (for downloadable files).

Going back to what I said earlier, people need to see something physical in order for them to comprehend what you are trying to show or tell them.

This is also one of the foundational ideologies that resulted in what Indians call "idol worship". In order for people to believe in God, the un-seeable, they needed to hold on to something physical – which is why idols and images and pictures of God were created.

Technically, God is everywhere. We could pray in front of anything - and nothing. Yet we don't. We need temples, mosques and churches, pictures and paintings and idols.

Disadvantages of Physical Products

Stephen Pierce, one of my "Guru Drona's", sold $888,817.49 worth of his smashing hit eBook "The Whole Truth" in one year - while probably spending less than 1% in doing so and pocketing 99% of the profits – something un-thinkable when you have a physical product.

There are multiple costs associated with the creation, procurement and sale of physical products – like the costs of manufacturing, shipping from manufacturer to retailer, inventory costs, shipping (to customer) and handling, and returning to inventory if there is a refund - just to name a few.

One of the biggest disadvantages of selling physical products is the overhead associated with shipping and handling. There is not really much you can do to reduce this overhead. Yes, you could negotiate with shipping companies, but it is preferable you stick with the reliable guys like the US Postal Services, UPS or FedEx.

Shipping continues to be the biggest overhead for most e-retailers - especially with customer fraud getting higher as it becomes easier to get a credit card, and even easier to get hold of someone else's credit card numbers. Fraud can be a really painful expense for businesses that rely on shipping products.

And fraud can cost even more if you are shipping overseas. Imagine spending $10 to ship a product from here to the Philippines, and after 30 days, your credit card processor not only reverses the purchase, but also levies an extra bank charge of $30.

So, you have lost the product itself, packing costs, shipping costs, all the time and effort that went into it, and then on top of it you have to pay about $30 in fines (reversal charges).

However, the good news is that fraud is only a fraction of your business. You should always account for 5%-10% of your business expenses as fraud-related (in retailing, it is even theft-related, commonly known as "pilferage").

If you work with your credit card processor to implement their various security features (like AVS – Address Verification System), and manually monitoring and tracking suspicious orders and even contacting the buyer before shipping the product, you will be able to minimize fraud to a big extent.

Advantages of Digital Products

Digital products do not have to be shipped. They can be downloaded instantly – which can be a huge incentive for those looking for instant gratification. This is especially true when it comes to information.

Someone who is stuck with a problem wants a solution now – right now – and not tomorrow, not in a few days, heck, they won't even wait for a few hours! They are willing to pay for it now, and they want the answer now.

Info-products are the perfect answer for such people. And digital products help fulfill this "instant" need for information. After all, they can download your product right off of your web site, as soon as they make the payment.

Nothing to be mailed: No shipping or handling fees to be collected. No going to the post office or sending stuff by courier. Everything is automated. You don't need to lift a finger to help complete the transaction. Buyer comes to your site, clicks on the "buy" button, pays by credit card, downloads product. End of transaction. You were not even required at any point.

Of course, you will always need to be there for pre- and post- sales support, and technical support and customer service, but you still did not have to participate in the actual sale for it to go through.

Now that's the power of digital products. Low (or no) overhead of delivery, shipping and handling. All of that gets added to your profits.

Disadvantages of Digital Products

Digital products are a double-edged sword. The fact that there's no shipping involved in the actual sale, means that there is no shipping involved in returns or refunds either!

In the real world, there is at least a 1% hesitation to ask for refunds or for exchanges, by someone who has purchased something either online or offline.

However, when it is a digital product, there is nothing to really return. All they need to do is to ask your payment processor (like ClickBank.com) for a refund, and they will be issued one, sometimes even before you hear about the actual request for a refund.

In other cases, they may file a complaint with your payment processor and say it was a fraudulent transaction, in which case again, the transaction is reversed by your payment processor, and on top of that, you may even be slapped with a substantial "chargeback" fee (sometimes about $30-$50!). So you not only lost the original sale, but also had to pay out of your pocket in fines.

But guess what, fraud and chargebacks still constitute a maximum of only about 5-10% of most businesses, and the remaining 90-95% is still a huge incentive to do business.

And fraud and chargebacks are going to happen regardless of whether your product is digital or not. It is a lot easier to digest when it is digital – because worst case, the buyer is still going to continue using your product even after getting a refund, but at least the goods did not come back damaged or used!

If it were a real product, you could end up losing the sale, the money paid in chargeback fees, as well as get back damaged goods which can not even be re-sold to anyone else!

So, fraud and chargebacks are much easier, not to mention less expensive to handle when it is a digital product.

The pertinent question here is, do you want to sell digital, or physical products?

5. How To Earn A Nice Little Paycheck From Google

Google's Adsense is such a big piece of the "making money online" puzzle that it deserves its own chapter.

Adsense is a Google service, where Google lets you place a piece of special "JavaScript" code on the pages of your web site, and when someone visits that page, based on the content on the page surrounding the ad (code), Google will determine in real time the type of ads that would be "relevant" to the content of your web page, and display the ads to your visitor.

You won't be able to sign up for Adsense till you have a working web site. So, for the information in this chapter to make sense, you must have a web site first, or at least a blog (try Blogger.com or Wordpress.com) that is up and running.

Sign up for an Adsense account at `Google.com/adsense` . It usually takes a few days for Google to approve your account. Once you are approved, you are now eligible to start placing Adsense ads on your web site.

To make money with Adsense, all it takes is...

- a decent web site with non-spammy content
- an Adsense account
- the will to continually develop more content, experiment, track results, and most importantly, and a willingness to treat even your little "hobby" site like an actual eBusiness!

Most people get stuck at Step #3. They put up a web site, they sign up for an Adsense account, simply slap on the Adsense tracking code on a couple of pages, and expect the cash registers to start ringing. And then, month after month, they go about complaining about how Adsense doesn't make money for them.

Online advertising is not dead. Adsense can - and does - make money for publishers. I myself make a *really* nice sum every month from Google, from ads on my various web sites. Adsense makes it very easy to monetize your content - be it a content web site, a blog, your online ezine, or a membership site. Google even provides you (the web site *publisher*) with a "heat map" that shows the most effective locations for placing the ads.

Google heat map

Google gives you guidelines on how certain locations for ads tend to be more successful than others. The "heat map" below illustrates these ideal placements on a sample page layout. See the image below - the colors fade from dark gray (which is truly a dark orange on their web site – meaning strongest performance) to light gray (truly light yellow when you see it in color). See the actual, colored heat map at:

`https://www.google.com/adsense/support/bin/answer.py?answer=17954`

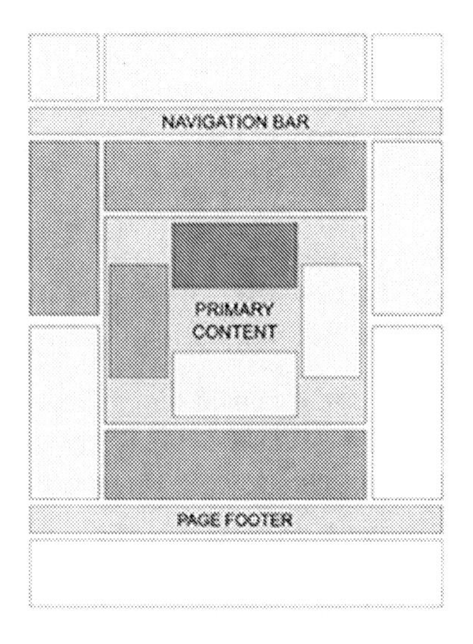

Google also publishes a blog dedicated to Adsense at `Adsense.Blogspot.com` (sidebar: when you sign-up for a free blogger.com account, you can too get a URL like yoursite.blogspot.com, or if you have an actual web site, you can setup your blogger account to publish the blog at a url on your site – like `blog.example.com`) as well as detailed help pages with tons of tips about how everything works, and what will fetch you the best results.

They publish success stories from other users who have been successful using Adsense, and it doesn't take much to follow the lead of those who have, and are experiencing success with Adsense ads.

The key to success with Adsense, as with anything else, to learn about what works, and then just implement it right away, while tweaking your specific implementation patters, and testing your individual results to make it more effective.

What works for one publisher doesn't work for everyone else. Like the famous disclaimer goes, "Individual results may vary". But there are a few general guiding principles which can get you started on the right foot and have you making money off of Adsense ads almost immediately.

Giving Adsense the Highest Priority

For Adsense to work, it is extremely important that you give Adsense ads the highest priority among all ads that you publish on a page.

Don't get greedy and surround your Adsense ads with 20 different affiliate links, flashing banners and distracting images and animations.

Yes, affiliate programs can make you a lot of money, but until you become an expert in affiliate marketing, Adsense ads will most definitely make more money for you – that is a given. To put it in a different way, it is easier to start making money with Adsense than it is with affiliate programs.

So forget about affiliate links for now; focus on Adsense, and the rewards will be quite generous.

Ads Above-the-Fold

"Above the fold" is a term coined by direct marketers. Online, this refers to the section of your web site that is visible when viewed in a web browser, without scrolling down. This is pretty much the top half of your web page, which is what the visitor sees as soon as they arrive at your web site.

Google's heat map (shown above) shows the different areas on your web site where the ads will be the most effective.

I cannot even begin to tell you the number of web sites I have visited that have Adsense ads practically hidden – they are published in such a location, that they wouldn't be visible unless you scrolled down the page once or twice, and even then, the ads would be buried in a dense jungle of affiliate links and banners, which would make it extremely hard to pick out even if someone were specifically looking for them.

The "What Does He Know" Factor

I have a childhood friend, who publishes a web site – and one day when he casually mentioned that he had been carrying Adsense ads for months and hadn't seen much revenue, I visited his web site and was shocked to see the terrible placement of the ads – I had to literally scroll down to the end of the home page, and had to practically "hunt" for it on the page– and finally there it was – in one of the worst performing formats that Google provides, with link and background colors that made it almost impossible for the visitor to see them, let alone click them.

If I myself had a hard time finding it when I was actually *looking* for it, how do you think a visitor - who is more interested in the content – would find it?

Obviously, it wasn't working. And over a period of the next few months, I repeatedly gave him some practical and powerful advice on improving his web site, his web pages, and on how to optimize his site for getting the most clicks on his Adsense ads.

But months later, and a number of chats and emails later, I found that he had still not implemented the changes I had recommended. And when I asked him why, he said he wasn't sure if they changes would really make a difference, and also that he had been busy with other stuff.

If I told you of a sure-fire way to make money and you are too busy to implement it, or don't care enough to at least try it and *test* it for yourself, especially when there's no costs or risks involved, then you really don't stand much of a chance at being successful.

This is the exact same mistake that 9 out of 10 publishers make – not listening to advice that they hear or read about, or too quick to judge what they read about, instead of trying it out and seeing if maybe it would work for them.

Either they are too lazy to implement it, or for many of them (especially with friends and family), the "What Does *He* Know" factor kicks in heavily, and they end up sabotaging any chance of success, by being stubborn in their approach.

This is also the same reason that millions of people around the world buy self-improvement books, courses, pay thousands of dollars to attend conferences and tele-seminars and one-on-one consulting, but only very few ever go on to do anything with what they've learnt or been given, let alone go on to become successful.

So, if you want to make money from Adsense, you have got to follow what I recommend here – and you have got to implement them, and tweak and test them continuously until you get the best possible results.

Optimizing Your Content

Probably the greatest innovation in online marketing was the ability to display *contextual ads* – which means, the ads that show up on a page are closely related to the content on your web page. This is "targeted marketing" at is best.

After all, if your site had content about PHP and JavaScript programming, what relevance would a "Women's Leather Shoes" advertisement have on your page? Almost *none*. The less relevant an ad is to your user, the less likely they will click on it – which means, the less likely that you will make money from that ad.

The key to Pay-per-click advertising is "relevance" – and Google rewards both advertisers and publishers for relevance.

For advertisers, the more relevant their ad is to the content (or keywords) that the user is looking for, the less they pay for their ads, and the higher their ad shows up when compared to the other advertisers competing in the same space.

For publishers, the incentive to make money is to get more people to their site – which means they would have to build a quality site with quality pages – and when the quality content triggers relevant ad, because the visitor is already looking for more information about that topic and has visited the site for that very reason, the more likely she is to click on an ad.

So it is a win-win-win for everyone.

Writing Copy To Trigger Better Ads

While this might sound like a sneaky tip, it is actually a well accepted formula for generating more revenue from your clicks.

Adsense ads, as you know by now, are triggered based on the copy of the page on which the ads are being displayed. So the copy on the page can be, and should be "influenced" (if you will), such that they trigger higher paying keywords.

Obviously, not every keyword generates the same kind of ads, and not all ads payout the same. So, as a copy writer, it is up to you (or whoever you hire to write the copy) to use substitution keywords in order to generate higher paying clicks. For example: the word "baby" may trigger different ads than the word "infant", "Teen" may differ from "Adolescent". There is no surefire formula that guarantees this.

There are tools like WordTracker (wordtracker.com) that can help you optimize your keywords, not only to increase your PPC payouts, but also to increase your ranking in the search engines. Quality tools like this come at a price, of course.

It does take some effort in experiment with different keywords, and constant tracking and monitoring of the copy changes as well as your earnings, to arrive at highly optimized copy.

It is *simple*, but not necessarily *easy*. But whoever said it would be?

Ad Formatting: Making Ads Appear "Unlike Ads"

When was the last time you clicked on a banner ad while you were online? You probably can't remember, if at all you did click on one.

That is because we have gotten too used to online ads. We are jaded by it, resulting in "ad blindness". We have gotten so used to it that we ignore it without even making an effort, without even realizing it.

Go to MSNBC.com, visit the business section, and click on an article or news item that interests you. Read through the entire article and try to notice how you automatically skim across the ads or anything that even appears like an ad. That's what the average person does online.

So the trick lies in making your Adsense ads appear *not* like ads. It is amazing how many web sites publish the Adsense ads right out of the box just as Google provides without customizing any of the colors or ad settings to their web site. It is bad enough that Google displays a conspicuous "Ads by Gooooogle" link under your ads. Why make it even more obvious that they are ads by making them stick out from your web site like a sore thumb?

So, here are a few tips to get you started.

Don't use borders; borders make it too obvious that it is an ad. Or maybe it may work in your favor, against all odds. You won't know this unless you try them both.

Make the background color, link color and text color of the ad the same as the background color, link color and text color of your web site. For example, if you site has a white background, blue links and black colored text, use the same colors for your ads too. That way, they will look like they are a part of your content.

Take advantage of all the formats that Google provides you with – link units, ad units, and the various sizes.

Sign up for Google's Adsense blog at `adsense.blogspot.com` and keep up with their posts.

Also study their web site that has tons of tips on using Adsense, at `Google.com/adsense/support`.

Ad Placement

Place your ads in places where people are likely to see them and more importantly, click on them.

Place your ads inline within your main content. Make your content flow *around* the ads.

See the Google Heat Map to see the best placement for the ads. But here are some other ideas you can use in conjunction to placement to help improve your CTR (Click-Through Rate – percentage of clicks versus impressions):

Switch Your Menu Location

People are used to seeing site menus on the left. Try switching them to the right, and place a 160x600 ad on the left. It will look like a menu, and you may get more clicks.

Now, don't think that this is tricking people into clicking on ads. What we're doing is not tricking people, but trying to get people click on a link because they want more information about a link they see on your site, and not because it is an advertisement.

Publishers know this very well, and welcome this strategy. Even Google welcomes it, and in fact publishes plenty of tips on how to make your ads "blend in" to your site.

This is a known and accepted evil. In fact, when people click on an ad without realizing it is an ad, then they are truly in "information gathering" mode, which means they are a "prospect" for the advertiser.

That's what the whole thing is about – getting "real prospects" to visit your web site or page, and take some action that will help you, the advertiser, sell them something.

Ads at the End of Every Article or News Item

When people are done reading an article or news item, they are usually at the bottom of the page where your content ended, and are now looking for where to go next. If your content continues on another page, there will usually be a "previous" or "next" link at the bottom of the article.

People have come to expect some links at the bottom of a page that will give them more content options to visit. They are in a "click-ready" mode at that point. Why not take advantage of that and place an ad unit at the bottom of every article? You're likely to get a lot of clicks from this section of your page.

Traffic

A lot of people get hung up just optimizing their ads, tweaking them over and over again, experimenting with new formats, sizes and colors, and forget the most important ingredient of a web site – the visitors!

Without traffic, even the most optimized Adsense web site in the world is worthless.

In the next chapter, let's see how to get traffic to your web site.

6. Traffic Generation

This is probably *the* most important chapter in this entire book.

Traffic is the lifeblood of a web site. Without traffic, the latest and the greatest of web sites will wither and die a slow and painful death.

When you have lots of traffic coming to your web site, you can test and experiment with your site's components – like site copy, headlines, conversion, stickiness, leads, sales, newsletter signups, downloads, and more.

More traffic almost always leads to more money, directly or indirectly. If you have lots of traffic and are not directly monetizing it through advertisement revenue or sales of products, you can always resort to one of the main things that high-traffic sites do: sell the site to a large corporation. If you can't monetize it, there are others who will pay you simply for the traffic that your site generates, even if your site doesn't make a single penny in profits.

Case in point: *YouTube*. Google purchased it for $1.65 billion even though they weren't making any profits, and weren't in fact making much revenue at all. But if you have traffic, then it means you are popular, and someone else can always find a way (or at least try) to monetize it.

However, creating a high traffic web site without a way of being able to use that traffic to multiply the traffic, is a wasted effort. If you have to shell out a lot of money for traffic, and aren't making any money, then that kind of traffic will benefit no one. However, if your traffic is free, then there is hope for whoever wants to buy you out.

Search Engine Optimization (SEO)

No one goes online thinking "Hmm, what is it that I can buy today?" (I guess there are a few exceptions there - like chronic shoppers, and insomniacs who buy stuff from late-night infomercials).

Seth Godin, in his ebook *Everyone Is An Expert* writes "...when you go online, you don't *search*. You don't even *find*. Instead, you are usually on a quest to *make sense*."

One thing you always have to remember is that people are *not* looking for *products* to buy – they are looking for answers to their questions, solutions for their problems; for someone to make meaning out of what they *think* they are looking for.

And the harder it is to find that meaning, the more they may be willing to pay for it, as long as it solves their immediate burning problem, is readily available all in one place, is easily readable, or answers all of their questions.

One of the most popular ways in which people find web sites, is through search engines.

The link of your web site is not going to just pop into your potential customer's head. They are either actively looking for sites like yours through a search engine, or you are putting information about your product into their head through advertising (even if it is word of mouth).

For many years now, it has been a common phenomenon where people just go online when they have a question. That question could be as simple as "what should I name my pet iguana" to "how to potty train my child" to something as important as "how do I save money for retirement".

With Google handling 50% (half) of the web's 5.6 Billion searches according to Nielsen//NetRatings (as of September 2006), it is becoming increasingly important to make ranking high on Google as your primary focus.

Yahoo and MSN are close behind in terms of searches handled, though Google by itself handles more searches than both these two giants put together.

With Google being the 800-pound gorilla in search, and the traffic they send you can pretty much make or break your ebusiness. So, a lot of the material provided her will be biased towards Google's terms and technology, and mainly about how to rank higher on Google.

Each of the above behemoths has a different way of calculating the importance of a web site or web page. The sites are then displayed in the search engine results pages (SERPs) in descending order of ranking. Paying attention to your own searching patterns and how you look for and find information the next time you are online, will probably make it obvious to you that most people do not go much further past the first couple of pages. In fact, most people won't even get past the first 3-4 links on the results page.

However, with millions of web sites competing for the same kind of keywords, it is no longer enough if you just appear in the top 3 pages; it is not enough if you appear *somewhere* on Page 1; it is not even enough if you appear in the top 5. You have *got* to be among the top 3 links, ideally at the #1 spot.

Any further below, and you can pretty much kiss the visitor good bye, which means you can kiss your profits good bye (at least from search engines). Of course, you will still get decent traffic from a popular search engine like Google by being *somewhere* on the first page of the results, but that will never be enough for you to make a decent amount of money from, say, PPC advertising.

The difference in traffic received by the first link is vastly more than the site that appears second. I have personally witnessed my site's traffic doubling (sometimes even more) in size by just moving up *one* position in the search results.

The art of "influencing" the ranking of your web site in the search engines, so as to appear higher in the search results is formally known as **Search Engine Optimization (SEO).**

There is a very *thin* line between "influencing" and "tricking" the search engines - if you do the latter, your site will be penalized at some point, and you will be dropped from the search engine's results. So, you've got to tread the SEO waters carefully.

Getting banned from (say) Google, could largely wreck any online business. So, it is very important that you quickly learn the difference between good-SEO (using "white-hat" techniques) versus bad-SEO (gray-hat or black-hat techniques used by spammers to artificially, but illegally boost the rankings of a site).

So, how exactly do you get a higher rank on these search engines?

The topic of SEO by itself merits an entire book. However, the only other way to do justice to this topic is to at least give this topic its own chapter, and hence this chapter.

How to Build Quality Content

Go ahead and repeat after me: "Content is KING".

Great original content is the most important factor in driving traffic. Without high quality content, your site will not be viewed as being high quality, which means your overall ranking (a.k.a. PageRank at Google) will suffer, which means you will show up lower in the SERP's compared to others who have a higher rank than your site.

Do not forget that with great content, you can also get your visitors to browse more, stay longer, opt-in to your newsletter(s), buy your product(s), and even click on your ads. Especially when working with Pay-per-click Ad providers like Adsense, the amount of traffic to your web site and the number of pageviews (pages viewed by your visitors) is kind of directly proportional to your Adsense earnings.

Do not ignore the importance of building great content that is genuinely useful and provides real value to your site visitors. Building pages just to appear higher in the SERP's will be considered as "spam", especially by

Google, and could end up with your web site getting banned from Google altogether.

There are many ways in which you can put up quality content on your site, and then follow some techniques (explained further below) to make sure your content is being noted by the search engines and various content directories.

Primarily, when you develop quality content, a lot of good things happen.

Firstly, the search engines love web sites that have lots of good, quality content. They also love sites that update their content frequently (like creating new articles or writing new blog posts). So the more you update your web site, the more you can get search engine spiders (software programs that visit your site and note your content and store it in the search engine's database) to visit your site more often, which again plays a role in getting higher ranking.

Secondly, when you create great content in your area of expertise, others will link to you, talk about you and blog about you. The more you get linked to, the more your "Incoming Links" count will improve. Which means your "Link Popularity" will increase.

Google for example, thinks of site "A" linking to site "B" as a "vote" from site "A" to site "B" – meaning, by linking to site B, site A is giving it a vote of confidence, saying "here is a site worth linking to", and giving its visitors a link to go check it out. The more such "votes" you get, the more popular your site is considered, which again leads to higher ranking.

Creating Original Content

The best way to build quality content and get brownie points from the search engines is to create your own original content. The only way you can establish yourself as an expert in your industry or domain, is by explicitly demonstrating, repeatedly, that you are indeed the expert you claim to be. And the only way to do this online, where your visitors can't see you face-to-face, is by writing a ton of original articles on the subject of your expertise, and publishing it not only on your web site, but also allow some of them to be published by others, while keeping your author info intact.

This is why people write books – to be considered as an expert. Note that the word "author" is the first half of the word "authority". When you become an *author*, you indirectly claim *authority* on the subject of your book, be it weight-loss, self-development, or financial advice.

The moment you write something from scratch, you are inherently granted copyright for the work. Of course, it's another thing that you still need to legally copyright it with your local government copyright agency if you want legal protection and empower yourself to go after infringers. Anyway, when you have your own copyrighted original content, there are many ways you can benefit from it:

- Create your own "niche" info-product that you can sell packaged as an e-book
- Use the content to create tele-seminars, write books, or even create audio products.
- Syndicate the content to other publications like web sites and magazines and radio and tv talk shows, for money and publicity.
- Syndicate the content to other web sites for money, or even for free along with the condition that they publish your "signature" or "author bio" at the end which will contain links to your sites and products, which is one of the biggest ways in which you can increase your link popularity.

The more content you have, the more pages you can create, which leads to more page views, which leads to more profits (in the form of clicks, leads or sign-ups).

What is a Blog?

If you don't know what a blog is, you are either very new to the web, or have been vacationing at a remote exotic location in Maui with no human contact.

Blogging is the art of being able to publish at the speed of thought. Blog software allows you to do this without having to worry about HTML, coding, maintaining an index of your posts, organizing and sorting. The software does everything except create the content.

That's where you come in, and provide meaningful and/or colorful commentary relevant to your target audience.

Every blogs must have a reason to exist - it could be just about keeping your friends updated about your life, or it could be as serious as blogging to create your individual brand, or it could be about getting people to vote for you.

Regardless of the intention behind it, blogs have become an extremely powerful medium to quickly spread your message, thoughts and ideas.

Google put blogs on the international map when they bought Blogger.com, the already popular free blogging service. Blogs played a big part in raising funds and spreading the message and brand and "tech-coolness factor" of the candidates during the 2004 US Presidential election. Blogs were published on what blogs are, how to publish blogs, and how to make money from your blogs.

There are both free and paid services available that host everything for you, and then there's both free and paid software, which you install on your web site. Here's a small list of what's available out there:

Hosted Services

Google's Blogger (blogger.com) is certainly the most popular free, hosted service. Other free blog services are Yahoo 360 (360.yahoo.com) and MSN Spaces (spaces.msn.com).

Typepad.com (Paid) is one of the more popular, commercial hosted services that charge a monthly fee.

Installed Software (Free)

`Wordpress.org`: This is what powers my own blog.

`Joomla.com`: A full-fledged CMS (Content Management System)

`Textpattern.com`: Another popular CMS

Publishing a Blog

A blog is a very powerful tool that gives you a platform to create original content and establish yourself as an expert. Think of it as your personal online journal - on steroids.

Blogs have become so powerful that bloggers are focusing on building subscribers for their blog's RSS/XML feed, rather than creating subscribers for their email newsletters.

As you know, excessive spam is spoiling email marketing for everybody - and as email providers come up with more and more techniques and filters for weeding out spam, many times it results in "false positives" being created (when your legitimate, double opt-in newsletter is flagged as spam). When that happens, your email will either be deleted, or will go into the "junk" or "bulk mail" folder, and your reader may never get to read it.

RSS feeds are way better in that context (of delivery), because you cannot force "feed" your blog's RSS "feed" to anyone. They will not see the feed unless they subscribe to it using a desktop- or web- based feed reader like LinkOverLoad.com or Google Reader (`Google.com/reader`).

Once you build up a substantial feed-subscriber-base, you can directly monetize your blog through ads, and the very fact that your blog is being read by a large audience means that you are considered an expert by many, could lead to other indirect benefits like better job offers, consulting opportunities, higher book sales or talk show appearances.

Also, good blog software like WordPress (what I use personally) makes it tremendously easy for the average person to create a well-structured, easily navigable site (your blog itself could be your main site), abstracting out all the technical details of having to know HTML, programming languages like PHP or knowing how to store and retrieve content from a database.

In fact, you don't even need a web site; simply head over to `WordPress.com` or `Blogger.com`, sign up for a blog just like you would sign up for free web mail, and start posting to your blog within the next 5 minutes.

Blogs are in fact a great way to get the search engines salivating, and come "spidering" your site, begging for more. We'll see more about that further ahead in this chapter.

Content Syndication

The fastest way to create content is to publish other people's content. This should be done with their permission of course. But due to the fact that authors get a lot of recognition, not to forget free incoming links to their web site when other people publish their articles, there are plenty of "syndication" (a.k.a. "free articles") sites out there that help authors and publishers to connect.

These article directories list thousands of free articles that you can publish on your site, as long as you follow the site's re-print policy. That usually involves publishing the article as-is, without making any changes, which also means printing the author's signature – the little blurb at the end of the article, which probably contains a link or two to the author's own sites. Thus, the author gets free incoming links to her site in return for giving you free content.

As you will read below, you will need to do the same in order to increase the PageRank of your site - you will need to write articles that other web site owners can publish on their site, thus getting you free incoming links.

As a site owner, it is not unusual to find yourself publishing others' content, as well as syndicating your own content.

Some of the popular article sites I use are `EzineArticles.com`, `GoArticles.com` and `ArticleCity.com`.

Just do a Google search on "free articles" or "free content" and you will see thousands of web sites that list such articles, all yours for the taking.

Note down the good ones as you visit them, as you will be going back there to submit your own articles for re-print by others. Of course, there is software available which will help you submit your articles to various article sites and directories, which we will see shortly.

RSS Feeds

Where there is a blog, there is a feed.

A RSS feed is simply a weirdly-formatted text file (actually, an XML file) that contains a summary of your blog's recent posts, complete with the post subject, url to the post, and sometimes even photos and the actual post's content.

This feed is automatically created if you use standard blogging software like WordPress or Blogger.

One of the best (not to forget, cheapest and fastest) ways to get free content for your web site, is to display a other people's RSS feeds. Every time the feed's content changes, content on your web site automatically changes, thus keeping the content fresh and ever-changing on your site.

Unfortunately, this technique is also used for illegitimate purposes. Sploggers (those who create *Splogs* - "**Sp**ammy **blogs**") often use it to generate thousands of "made for Adsense" pages, whose primary purposes are either to increase PageRank, or to get people to click on to the site, and leave by clicking on Adsense (or other PPC) ads.

But if you use it for legitimate purposes, you will find that publishing RSS feeds on your site can be a great way to provide targeted, complementary content for your visitors.

Magpie (`Magpierss.sourceforge.net`) is a great open-source PHP script that will allow you to easily publish any third-party RSS feed on your site. I have tried out many RSS scripts, but haven't found any as good as Magpie. I have used it this script to create a pretty cool web-based feed-aggregator service at `LinkOverLoad.com`, a la Google Reader and Google Personalized home page.

Getting Your Site Indexed

When a search engine adds your site's URL (Uniform Resource Locator – a.k.a. *link*) to its database, it means the search engine "indexed" your site. This means, that when someone searches for keywords closely matching the content on your web site, you will show up in the results.

Getting indexed doesn't mean your site will show up on the first page of search results - it just means your site will be listed somewhere in the potentially hundreds of thousands (if not millions) of search results returned.

Like we saw before, if you are not in the top 3 spots on a search page, you probably won't make much money (from free search engine traffic, of course).

For now, let us learn the fastest way to get indexed on a search engine, because getting indexed is obviously the first step to achieving a higher ranking.

Blog-and-Ping

This is arguably the fastest possible way for a spanking new site to get indexed in search engines.

"Blog and Ping" is a term that refers to a technique where you make a post on your blog, and using your blog software's built-in feature, you send out a "ping" to various blog directories and blog-search engines, notifying them that you have made a new post on your blog.

A ping is nothing but a signal sent from *your* blog (the pinger) to the *target directory or search engine* (the pingee); this signal primarily contains the link to your post.

Following this *ping*, the pingee picks up the link and content from your post, and when someone on that site searches for keywords contained in your post, then your post shows up in their search results.

Search engines (especially Google) love blogs, because blogs are full of "useful" content (at least they are supposed to be). The more active your site is - in terms of frequent, new content - the better your ranking will be.

One day in November 2006, I logged into my Google Adsense account, and my jaw dropped when I saw that my Adsense earnings from one of my major sites had dropped 80% - meaning, I had made only 20% of what I had been making every day. I hurried over to Google, searched for my primary keywords, and saw that my site had suddenly dropped more than a few notches, from position #2 to a measly position #8 in Google's SERP (search engine results pages). Now, Google sends me about 80% of my total traffic to this site. So, as soon as my site dropped to #8, it went "below the fold" (meaning, out of the view of the first part of the results page that appears when you do a search, without having to scroll down). No wonder that my Adsense earnings dropped about 80% too!

Sidebar: That just goes to show you that even having a "top 10" listing on Google (or any search engine for that matter) doesn't really do much good, because apparently not many people look beyond the first 2 or 3 links, especially if those top few sites give the user what they are looking for, or lead them on to other things from there on - so the user may never come back to Google to look further below.

I wasn't sure what caused this to happen, but I quickly made some adjustments on the site, moved some stuff around, published some new content on my main site and on my blog, pinged all directories that I am aware of, removed some external links that I suspected might have triggered some Google-spam-filter, and also used Google's SiteMap tool to ping Google of my changes to my main site, and within 48 hours (yep, that fast), my site was back to position #2. God bless Google!

So, pinging is a pro-active way of letting other sites know that you have made some changes on your site or blog.

Especially with Google, when you ping them using the sitemap tool, you can see how quickly Googlebot (Google's spider) comes knocking. This is especially useful in situations like my scare-scenario above, where I hurriedly made some changes, wanted Google to know right away that I had indeed made some changes, and wanted my changes to be considered when calculating my ranking the next time around.

Well, that is exactly what happened – Google seemed to like my changes (or just the fact that I had made some changes), got brownie points for being a "good publisher", and gave me my Adsense earnings back.

Moral of the story: Never fudge with Google - not if you are making any money at all from Adsense.

Be a "ethical publisher", publish often, publish white-hat, build quality content, and *The Big G* will reward you with Adsense dollars.

What to Ping?

Further below in the next section, you will find a list of URL's that I have in my own WordPress-driven blog (login as *admin*, go to *Options* > *Writing* > (Scroll down to) *Update Services*).

Every time I "Publish" a post, WordPress automatically saves the entry first, and then pings each of these URL's in succession, until it has gotten back a (successful, or a 'time-out') response from each one.

Pinging all these URL's can be very slow and take about 5 minutes, so do not freak out and hit 'cancel' or close the browser window, as that will stop the pinging from completing.

Store this ping list online (I use both Yahoo Notepad (`notepad.yahoo.com`) and Google Notebook (`google.com/notebook`) for storing such notes) and then enter it in the "Update Services" section of your WordPress blog setup. Do this only when you are writing a new post, and are about to "publish" it.

Once you're done publishing the post, remember to go back to the "Update Services" section clear the list and save the change. Here's why - once you have "published" a post, if you still let the ping list remain in your blog setup, then every time you make a change to any published post (correcting a typo, adding a link to your post, or changing the ad code), WordPress will once again ping all of the URL's listed with the same post.

If you make multiple posts a day, or go back to an older post and make some edits, make sure you are pinging only once or twice a day by selectively adding and removing the ping-list from your blog setup. Ping any more than that, and you may get banned by the service for abusing the privilege.

Pinging Google

You cannot ping the main Google search engine using the ping list below – the list only contains the ping URL for Google's blog-search (`blogsearch.google.com`) service.

If you want to ping Google (the search engine, and not the blogsearch service) about changes to your blog as part of your main site, then use the **Google Sitemap Plugin for WordPress Blogs** available at (`Arnebrachhold.de/2005/06/15/google-sitemap-generator-for-wordpress-25`) using which you can create an XML file with your blog posts, and ping Google. Of course, you must have signed up for a Google Sitemaps account first and added your blog to that account.

However, if you are just making changes to your main web site and not your blog (assuming your main web site and your blog are not the same, or if your main site not powered by WordPress), then use the **Google Sitemap Tool for** (non-Wordpress) **Web Sites** available at (`Enarion.net/google/phpsitemapng/`) to create your sitemap XML file and ping Google.

So here's what the ping list looks like:

http://blogsearch.google.com/ping/RPC2
http://rpc.pingomatic.com/
http://rpc.technorati.com/rpc/ping
....
....

http://api.moreover.com/RPC2
http://ping.feedburner.com
http://api.feedster.com/ping

The entire list is available online for you to copy-paste, at: http://ravisrants.com/2006/12/29/the-ping-list-how-to-make-google-your-little-bee-yaach/

Remember, all it takes is just one ping a day to get Google to come crawling (literally *and* figuratively) your web site.

Tag-and-Ping

Tag-and-Ping is very similar to Blog-and-Ping.

In Blog-and-Ping, all you are doing is notifying a site that you have published a post, and letting the site know about your post's URL, heading and content of your post. But with Tag-and-Ping, you can explicitly notify a site (like Technorati.com) how your post is classified, what the keywords are that are associated with your post, and under what keyword searches (on say, Technorati.com) your blog post should show up.

Many sites like `Technorati.com`, `Furl.net` and `Flickr.com` send out their spiders crawling for content that have "tags" pointing to their sites. Tags are nothing but human-defined categories – so a blog post that says "How to make money with Google Adsense" could be tagged under the categories "Google" and "Adsense". So, when you create, say, Technorati Tags (the site will give you code to create a tag) called "Google" and "Adsense" and ping Technorati.com's ping server, then when a Technorati user searches their site for the keywords "Google" or "Adsense", then your post will show up in the search results

Tags are a great way for both creators of content, and the readers of the content, to classify content under a category.

Blog software like WordPress allows automatic tagging of posts when you publish a post under a certain category. For example, in my blog `RavisRants.com`, I have created categories like "Adsense", "Adwords", "Apple" and "Google", among others. When I publish a post about Adsense, I check both the "Google" and "Adsense" categories under which to save the post. When I "Publish" the post, WordPress automatically pings all the directories that I have listed in my blog setup.

Also, with WordPress, you don't have to specifically create tags for Technorati, Furl or other sites. As long as you have listed your post under a category, WordPress will automatically create tags for you with the same name as your post's categories, and ping the sites with these tags.

Google SiteMaps

Everything Google does, they are usually the first to do it, or at least the first to do it differently and they do it remarkably well.

Google has a web-based service called "SiteMaps" located at http://Google.com/webmasters/sitemaps/

Before SiteMaps, when you created a new page on your site, or updated your existing pages, there was no way of pro-actively letting Google (or any search engine for that matter) know that you have new or updated pages. So, the search engine result pages would continue to show outdated information (for example, you may have changed your page title or description, yet your old page title and description still keep showing up on the search results).

Google was one of the first search engines to automate the process of adding web sites to their database (called "index"). So, Google's software (a.k.a the "spiders") would go from site to site following the links on each web site, and crawl more sites in the process, and add all of the information to Google's index.

Also, whenever you added Google services to your web site (like say, using Google Adsense) on your site, you could see Google's robots hitting your site within minutes of putting the ad code on your pages.

In the beginning, Google's spiders used to come crawling your web site and update information about any new or modified pages, about once a month. Then, as the number of web sites in Google's index started growing larger, the time period between successive crawls started getting longer and longer and eventually got to a stage that it took practically months for your web site changes to show up on Google.

But that was before SiteMaps. Once Google introduced SiteMaps, they turned the entire search industry on its head – now, a web master could make a change to her web site, create a specially formatted file (an XML file) and notify Google about the creation of this new file, which had details about which pages had changed, how often they change, etc.

So, instead of sitting around for Google's spiders to come to your web site when they got done with the billions of other sites in the world, you could now pro-actively inform Google that you have made changes to your site. And once you notified Google of the changes, you could see the Google spider crawling your site within hours, and then within days of that happening, you could see those changes reflected in Google's search results.

Also, once you add your site to Google SiteMaps, Google will display a lot more sensitive information to you (the site owner) about your site than is available to an outsider. Information like the top keywords used to find your site, the ranking of your site for various keywords, the PageRank of various pages of your site, unreachable (or broken) links on your site will be extremely valuable when it comes to "optimizing" your web site to get a higher ranking.

Get more information about sitemaps by going to:

http://Google.com/support/webmasters/bin/topic.py?topic=8465

Blog-and-Bookmark

Using Digg, Del.icio.us, Reddit and StumbleUpon

Once you create a new article, page or post on your blog or web site, you can submit the link to hugely popular sites like Digg.com, Reddit.com, Del..icio.us and StumbleUpon.com to further actively popularize your content. These sites are frequented by a large number of visitors – primarily web surfers looking for information – be it technical, entertaining, educational or controversial.

These sites have the ability to vote on content that they find to their liking. So, if your article or post connects with these users, and if a large number of users vote for (on digg.com, voting for a site is called as "digg"ing a site – as in, "I dig(g) your site"), then you could get a huge surge of visitors within hours of posting your article there.

In fact, the home pages and category home pages of these sites are so popular and visited by such a highly targeted group of folks, that a large amount of traffic from these sites can literally bring your server to its knees (yet another reason why you need a good web host like hostrocket.biz or dream-host.biz).

These sites also give you "badges" that you can publish along with your post, that says "Digg this" or "Add to Technorati". However, with the number of content aggregators becoming large, it is hard to keep track of all of these sites and publish that many buttons on your site, which not only looks ugly, but will also take up too much precious real estate. You can use services like `AddThis.com` or `FeedButton.com` that give you a single button using which your reader can then go on and bookmark your site, or add your RSS feed to any feed reader of her choice. See my own blog RavisRants.com for ideas.

To be able to utilize these sites effectively, you have to use the site for a while, visit the forums, and see what kind of people hang out at these sites, and see if they fit your web site's theme. For example, Digg and Reddit users are generally geeks and very web savvy, youngish people. However, Slashdot may have a slightly more serious and mature audience.

What becomes popular on one site, may completely flop on the other. The users of these sites are also very competitive. So, for example, any legitimate, meaningful article that favors one versus the other may not do so well on the site that is being put down.

Submitting Your Site

Another common way to get into search engines and directories is to go to each of these sites, look for the section where they allow you to "submit" the URL of your home page, and then fill out a little form. Following this, the site's software (*spider* or *robot*) or humans (editors) will add your site to their database.

This process can take a while, and some, like Yahoo! even expect a one-time and/or a recurring annual payment, to guarantee or expedite the inclusion.

But as long as you use the *Blog-and-Ping* method, and also submit your site manually to the big guns like Google (50% search share), Yahoo (30%) and MSN (10%). Don't worry about the other search engines, as these three giants together handle close to 90% of the web's search traffic, and are the ones who will send you almost all of your search engine traffic (with the exception of `Dmoz.org`), and also because being listed with them could also mean getting listed on other major sites (for example, AOL uses Google's search results).

There are both software and services available that offer to submit your site to thousands of search engines and directories, but stay away from using them, because it could end up doing more harm than good for your site.

The main ones you should submit to right away (with the link to the "submit" page also given below) are:

Google: **Google.com/addurl**

MSN: **Search.msn.com/docs/submit.aspx?FORM=SUNO**

Yahoo: **Search.yahoo.com/info/submit.html**

DMoz (Human-powered directory): **DMoz.org**

Increasing PageRank™

Like we saw earlier, getting indexed is not the same as getting ranked highly in the Search Engine Results Pages (SERPs). You have to appear in the top 3 spots, or at worst, somewhere on the first page of the SERPs to get any meaningful traffic at all from search engines.

Once you get a high ranking for your keywords, you will get a lot of free traffic from search engines; you simply cannot beat this form of traffic because it can be huge in numbers, and it is free! So, you must focus and put in a lot of effort in getting your site highly ranked, as other means of traffic can be a lot more work, not to mention, very expensive too.

What is PageRank

As defined at Google.com/technology:

---------<Start-quote-from-Google>-------
"Google runs on a unique combination of advanced hardware and software. The speed you experience can be attributed in part to the efficiency of our search algorithm and partly to the thousands of low cost

PC's we've networked together to create a superfast search engine.

The heart of our software is PageRank™, a system for ranking web pages developed by our founders Larry Page and Sergey Brin at Stanford University. And while we have dozens of engineers working to improve every aspect of Google on a daily basis, PageRank continues to provide the basis for all of our web search tools.

PageRank Explained

PageRank relies on the uniquely democratic nature of the web by using its vast link structure as an indicator of an individual page's value. In essence, Google interprets a link from page A to page B as a vote, by page A, for page B. But, Google looks at more than the sheer volume of votes, or links a page receives; it also analyzes the page that casts the vote. Votes cast by pages that are themselves "important" weigh more heavily and help to make other pages "important."

Important sites receive a higher PageRank, which Google keeps track of, each time it conducts a search. Of course, important pages mean nothing to you if they don't match your query. So, Google combines PageRank with sophisticated text-matching and content-analysis techniques to find pages that are both important and relevant to your search. Google goes far beyond just counting the number of times a term appears on a page, and examines many aspects of a page's content (and the content of the pages linking to it) to determine if that page is a potential match for your query.

Integrity

Google's complex, automated methods make human tampering with our results extremely difficult. And though we do run relevant ads above and next to our results, Google does not sell placement within the results themselves (i.e., no one can buy a higher PageRank). A Google search is an easy, honest and `objective way to find high-quality websites with information relevant to your search. "`

-----------<**End-quote-from-Google**>-------

There are two ways in which you can optimize your site to increase your PageRank: On-page Optimization and Off-page Optimization.

But before you get into that, the first tool you need to arm yourself with is to get a version of the FireFox browser that includes the Google Toolbar. I cannot recommend FireFox highly enough, because there are a lot of tools available that will help you as a site owner – from page analysis to shortcuts to information management. So, install the Google tool bar, and enable the "PageRank" and "Information" tabs.

When you have the PageRank (PR) tool enabled, you will be able to see the PR of every site you visit, as you surf the web. PR is shown as a green bar (also popularly known as "Green Gold") on a scale of 1 to 10. The higher the number, the higher the PR, and the higher a site will show up in a search. So, a web site with PR7 will *almost always* show up higher than a similar web site with PR6. I say *almost always* because there are a few exceptions to this rule which we will go into later, but for now, just know that one of your main goals as a web site owner is to constantly keep working on increasing your PR.

The Google Sandbox

When you first launch your site, Google is believed to put your site into what is popularly called as the "Google Sandbox". This is also called as the "Supplemental Index" (explained further down in this chapter).

When your site is first indexed (it appears in the search results when perform a Google search on just your domain name– `Example.com`), it won't show any PageRank for a while. It could take even months for you to see any PageRank at all for your site – it usually remains at 0 (zero – which means the PageRank tool in Google toolbar shows no bar at all) until one day you will miraculously see a PR of anywhere between 1 and 3 appear.

It is popular belief that Google puts all new sites in a sandbox so as to make sure spammers don't suddenly launch sites with thousands of incoming links and then spam the search results which would break the integrity of Google's results.

So, don't be alarmed if your site initially doesn't show up on Google for a while, or when it does show up, if it doesn't have any PR. During this time, you should start an incoming-link-building campaign, because even if your site has been online for months, if there are no incoming links to your site, Google will not assign you PR.

PageRank is a very precious commodity. In fact, when you start exchanging links with other sites, if you have a high PR for your links page (`Example.com/links.html` - where you would normally publish the links of those who you are trading links with), it is a lot easier to convince other sites to exchange links with you, because your high PR has a positive effect on all the sites that you link to.

The higher the PR of a site that is linking to you, the more your web site's PR will benefit from the linking. So, loosely stated, one link from a PR 10 web site is probably worth a hundred links of PR 1. This is an inference from the guidelines offered by Google, and the example is not meant be taken literally).

PageRank Influence and Bleeding

PageRank gets transferred from one site to another. In other words, the PR of the linking site has an influence on the eventual PR of the linked site. So, like I mentioned above, you get more credit for a PR10 site linking to you than a PR9, and so on downwards. The higher the PR of the site is that is linking to you, the better.

So, if you have a page, say `index.html`, on your site that has PR5, then every outgoing link on that page – even to your own internal pages - will benefit from its PR. But the flip side of the coin is that the more outgoing links there are on this page, the more diluted will be the influence of this page's PR on each of the outgoing links, because the influence is spread across many links.

So, to preserve PR and prevent what is known as *PageRank Bleeding*, it is in your best interest to publish as few outgoing links as possible from each page.

Now, this does not mean that you shouldn't link to pages in your own site. It just means that you should use outgoing links with caution, and be aware of this *PR bleeding* phenomenon when you publish links to third-party web sites.

Thankfully, a while ago, Google introduced a powerful new feature, called the "nofollow" tag.

Rel=NoFollow

This is where you add an extra attribute to the `<a href..>` tag:

```
<a href="http://www.Example.com" rel="nofollow">Link
Text</a>
```

So, even though you have published a link to `Example.com`, the "nofollow" tag informs Google (and any other search engine that supports this tag) to not pass on any PR influence to this link (which has the "nofollow" attribute in the `<a href=..>` tag, as shown above).

Using this tag, you are effectively preventing the distribution of your precious PageRank to this link, and in effect preserving your PageRank for possibly other links of your choice (that do not have this attribute in the `<a href..>` tag).

So, this way, you can pick and choose which pages on your own site or external sites should benefit from your linking, and which ones shouldn't.

When doing a link exchange, the whole idea is that the *linkee* should benefit from the *linker*'s PR. So, it is usually not acceptable in a link exchange to use the "nofollow" tag. Similarly, in the case of article syndication, many article exchange sites specifically mention in their policy that the publisher may not use this tag when linking to the author's site, because the whole purpose of the author writing an article and allowing you to publish it for free on your site is to gain incoming links and increase link popularity.

On-Page Optimization

On-page optimization is in your control – this is what you do with each and every page of your web site.

This is where you use various best practices and standards in creating your web pages, naming your pages, and in creating the content of the page. You can make frequent changes, experiment with various techniques as often as you want, and track the results.

It will help you a lot in the long run if you completely absorb, maybe even memorize, all of the SEO techniques and strategies mentioned in this chapter, so you can keep them in mind every time you create a new page on your web site.

Following these patterns when creating a new web site is a whole lot easier, and will save you a whole lot of time and heart-ache later, rather than doing it wrong the first time and trying to re-factor your entire site later.

Creating a Human-Friendly Site

While it is certainly very important to keep all the SEO factors in mind when designing and developing a web site, the one factor that you cannot, and must not overlook, is that web sites are ultimately consumed by humans, not machines.

SEO is just one of the many tools available to help influence the ranking of your site so that more people can find it among millions of web sites. But focusing all of your time, money and efforts on optimizing your site for the spiders and letting the ball drop on creating great content, is the biggest mistake most web site owners make.

Google urges web site owners to "Make pages for users, not for search engines"[2]; I couldn't agree more. SEO is just a means to an end, not the end goal of your web site. The ultimate goal is to create a high-quality web site that offers great content to your visitors, answers their questions, solves their problems, or simply helps them further along in whatever their quest is; and giving your visitors what they want is the only thing that will eventually lead to other desirable outcomes - like your visitors clicking on your ads, buying more of your products or services, recommending your site to others.

Creating a Search Engine-Friendly Site

Keyword density, positioning and Meta-tags

It is very important that your keywords appear in your *page title*, not just for ranking purposes, but also for marketing. In the search engine results pages (SERPs), the title of your page is what a web surfer will see, which appears as a highlighted link (with the link pointing to your actual web page), below which she will see the content from your page's "description" meta-tag.

Having your target keywords in your page title and description is extremely important, because search engines (especially Google) uses a combination of these two, along with your PageRank, keyword density and relevance to determine how high you rank in the SERPs.

It can also help a lot to have the keywords in your page name itself - and if possible, in your domain name too. While it is not an absolute requirement to have the keywords in your domain name, it certainly

---

[2] See Google's Webmaster Central site at: Google.com/support/webmasters/bin/answer.py?answer=35769

helps, because in the end, all other things being equal (like PageRank), subtle factors like this one can help break the tie.

Google is not so crazy about "Keyword Density" (the number of many times a keyword appears on your page), and in fact might even penalize you if it finds the same set of words repeated too many times, and Google also discounts the content of your meta-tags, but other engines like Yahoo still give meta-tags and keyword density a lot more importance then Google.

Google gives a lot (and I mean a *lot*) of weight to link popularity, link text and relevance/context of the 3rd party web pages that are linking to your site, whereas other search engines don't care as much about the external factors. It is fair to generalize that Google leans more towards off-page factors while Yahoo and other engines lean more towards the on-page factors.

It is extremely important to have your primary keywords within a <H1> heading tag, right at the top of the page, preferably not embedded within a complex HTML table structure. You can use the <H2> (slightly smaller) heading tag for your sub-heading, which should contain a further sprinkling of your primary and/or secondary keywords.

These tags are the ones at the top of your web page's source code and look something like `<Meta.../>`

There are many *meta-tags* available, like "title", "keywords", "description", and many more. Some of these tags are ignored by many of the more popular search engines, but the "title" and "description" tags do make a difference. For example, in a Google search, the search result for each site shown is the title of the page as the link, and the description is used to give a short summary to the searcher. If Google cannot find a good match in your description, it will use a random combination of text from your web page that contains the key words used by the searcher.

Just do a Google search for "baby potty training" and study each of the links in the results. Note down the link and description shown by Google, follow the link to the site, view the source (right-click, then click "view source") and try to analyze the meta tags on the page versus the text shown by Google.

If the visitor searched for "php scripts" and your page title also contains the words "php scripts", and if your site has a lot of content about "php" and "scripts", then you can get a pretty high ranking.

Text-Based Content

Make sure your content is in plain text (HTML *is* text) and not inside some image or Flash animation, because the search engines cannot read anything that's not text (with the exception of PDF and MS Word docs); and what they cannot read, they cannot analyze.

Keyword Density

If your site has a lot of content of baby names, has the words "baby" and "names" in the domain name itself, or in the name of the web page, mentions the words "baby" and "names" to a reasonable extent in the content, then there's a good chance you will show up higher than most other sites.

But keep in mind that overdoing the same can get you into trouble for spamming. So, you've got to find the right balance for not just this one, but for all SEO techniques.

Internal Linking Structure

It is very important how you internally arrange and link to your various pages on your site. Do not have cryptic page names – try to have more meaningful names, maybe even separated by hyphens, to make it easy for the search engines to decipher what the page is about.

For example, your page name on car buying tips could be `Example.com/car-buying-tips.html` , which is a lot more descriptive than `Example.com/cbt.html` or `Example.com/cars.html`.

The first version has many advantages – one of them is that it will rank higher than the latter ones when someone is searching for, say `car buying tips`, because the keywords in the search will match the name of your page. Now, it is not fully known whether `car-buying-tips.html` would rank much higher than `carbuyingtips.html`. But since it's not like someone is going to type in your page name from memory, it doesn't matter if the page name itself has hyphens or not.

However, it is altogether a different discussion about having hyphens in your domain name itself (see the section on domain names earlier in the book), but just know that it won't cause your visitor any difficulty whatsoever if your page names are longer than usual, and have hyphens in them.

The second advantage of having such hyphenated- and longer- page names is that contextual ad networks (like Google Adsense) will pick up on the context of the page faster, and will deliver better ads more relevant to your page's theme.

If you had named your page simply as `cars.html`, you could get a wide range of ad topics, like ads about how to assemble a car, driving schools, buying auto parts, donating cars, or repairing cars – none of them having anything to do with *buying* cars.

Advertisers prefer more narrowly targeted pages (like `car-buying-tips.html` versus a generic `cars.html`) because their conversion generally tends to improve with a narrowly targeted audience. The more highly targeted the ads are to your content, then the higher click-throughs you will get, which means the more you will earn.

Also, since the automated bot is able to read car-buying-tips.html more easily than carbuyingtips.html (which could be read as *carb .... tips* – with *carb* as in *carbohydrates*) you will start seeing the right kind of ads displayed on your site right from impression one, when you first upload the page to your site and visit it yourself.

If the ad network cannot make out the context of your page either from the file name, domain name or the content of the page, then you will probably see completely irrelevant ads (in the above example, if it reads the text as *carb*, then you may see health, dieting and fitness related ads).

In fact Adsense will even display public service ads (that won't earn you any money) on your site, if it cannot determine to a reasonable extent the context of your web page, or if your site is in the sandbox (you can configure it to show a custom image instead of public service ads.)

Using Rel=NoFollow For Your Own Pages

As we saw before, the "rel=nofollow" tag can be a great tool in selective distribution of PageRank. You can use the nofollow tag to prevent PR bleeding of your own page, when it is necessary to link to a third-party web site for the sake of reference, but you do not wish to pass on your own page's PR to this third-party site.

This strategy is not very useful when exchanging links, but it can be very useful say, in a blog – where you want to link to an external site as part of your post; this link may be because you are referring to, commenting about, or adding to the content on an external site, and just because you are passing on the link and the traffic doesn't mean you have to give up PageRank too. In such situations, you can use the nofollow tag on all outgoing links from your blog's content.

The *nofollow* tag can also be very useful in an unusual situation – like when linking to your own pages on your site (internal links). Why exactly would you prevent your own pages from getting PageRank influence, you ask?

Here's why: Let's say your home page is the highest PageRank'ed page on your site. Now your home page may have outgoing links to many internal pages of your web site. Some of them may be less valuable than the others, in terms of getting your site ranked in the search engines.

Your home page will link to pages on your site just so that humans can navigate to those pages - for example, your `aboutus.html` page or your `press.html` page don't necessarily need to rank very high, because these page exist to give more information to visitors who are already on your web site. Those are not the ones which are going to lead new traffic to your site.

So, you don't have to waste your home page's precious PageRank to these "For Your Information" pages – like `aboutus.html`, `support.html`, `contactus.html`, `privacy.html`, `terms.html`, `links.html` (the page that contains the actual HTML code that potential link partners should use in a link exchange), `faq.html` and others.

You can use the *nofollow* tag for these FYI pages, and choose which important pages (or category hubs) of your web site should get the PageRank influence from your home page, and link to just those *without* using the *nofollow* tag.

Blogs: Naturally SE Friendly

Blogs, because they are naturally a content-management tool, organize your content and navigation and internal linking in such a way that they are by default search engine-friendly. The page names are usually a hyphenated version of the heading of your blog post, pages are automatically archived and linked to, you can publish a single post under multiple categories which means when the search engines spider your site, they will find the same post through multiple unique URL's which will also improve your page count.

There are also many tools and plug-ins available – like for blog-and-ping, tag-and-ping, auto blog-posting, book-marking, automatic RSS feed generation from your blog posts and comments, and Google sitemap generation which make it very easy to notify search engines and content aggregation sites about your new blog post, which means your content will get spidered faster and available in search results faster to the outside world.

Also, many search engines do not, or can not spider URL's with a "?" in them (also called as a "query string"). Most blogs come with feature of being able to do *URL Rewriting* (the creation of SE-friendly url's).

So instead of the uglier and harder-to-spider URL:

```
Example.com/blog?post=273&year=2007&month=10
```

...the URL becomes the more SE and Ad service friendly:

```
Example.com/blog/2007/10/car-buying-tips/
```

Off-Page Optimization

Off-page optimization refers to all of the factors that are beyond your web site – things that you cannot directly control (but can influence, as we will see), like incoming links, link text of those incoming links, the relevancy of the linking site when compared to yours, PageRank of the linking site, and so on.

Off-page optimization plays as much a big role in getting a higher PR as On-page optimization. The only difference is it is a lot harder to achieve, and could take a while to implement and see the results, as these external factors are not under your control.

Link Popularity

This is probably the most important part of off-page optimization. Search engines like Google give a lot of importance to how important your web site is. One of the ways they measure this, is to count how many other web sites link to your site. If a large number of sites are "mentioning" your site and/or are linking to your site, then it obviously it means you have something worth writing about, and linking to.

Even though this concept is abused by sites referred to as "link farms" that generate thousands of bogus inward links to the main site just to improve link popularity, these generally get deleted from the search engine's index once they are caught, and the site could even get banned for life.

So, if you are putting up genuine content and the links are genuine, then your page rank will get a big boost over a period of time.

To find out how many sites are linking to you, go to Google and search for:

```
link:Example.com
```

You will see a list of incoming links from all sites, including pages from within your own site. If you don't see anything, then it means that you probably haven't been assigned PageRank yet.

If you simply want to see all the pages in your site that are currently indexed in Google, search for:

```
site:Example.com
```

[More Google search tips in the section *Google Hacks* further ahead.]

Building link popularity is such an integral part of your web site's success, that it deserves its own chapter (See next chapter, "Link Popularity").

Link Text and the "Home" Syndrome

It is not only important to get incoming links to improve PageRank, but the "link text" of those incoming links also plays a huge role in getting a high PR. This "link text" is the actual text that links to your page or site.

For example, consider the following lines of code:
Link #1:
<a href=http://www.Example.com>Example.com</a>

Link #2:
<a href=http://www.Example.com>Car Buying Tips</a>

As you can probably guess, link #2 is far more powerful, and will get you a higher PR than link #1. This is because the first link's "link text" does not contain the key words relevant to your web site, but the second one does.

For a site visitor, link #2 will make more sense, and is more descriptive of what your site or page is about – and there is a higher chance of them clicking on it if they are really looking for tips on car buying. However, link #1 doesn't say anything about your site. Unless your keywords that you are promoting are also available in the domain name itself, the link text doesn't really say what your site is about.

Anything that is good for the user is good for Google. Google loves such nuances, and does a lot to keep the integrity of its search engine very high, and focuses a lot on usability and usefulness of content.

So, because link #2 is more useful for the user, Google gives you more points for incoming links that look like link #2.

Here's proof that link-text actually matters: Search for the word "home" on Google. The results will look similar to the screenshot below.

As you can see, the New York Times web site, `nytimes.com` is the #1 listing in the search results. Is this because the site has anything to do with a "home"? Nope! This is because it has a very large number of inner pages that all point to the home page using the text "home", and a combination of the large number of incoming links, link-text influence, and generally high PageRank of the overall web site due to a number of third-party web sites linking to it's home page, various news stories and articles.

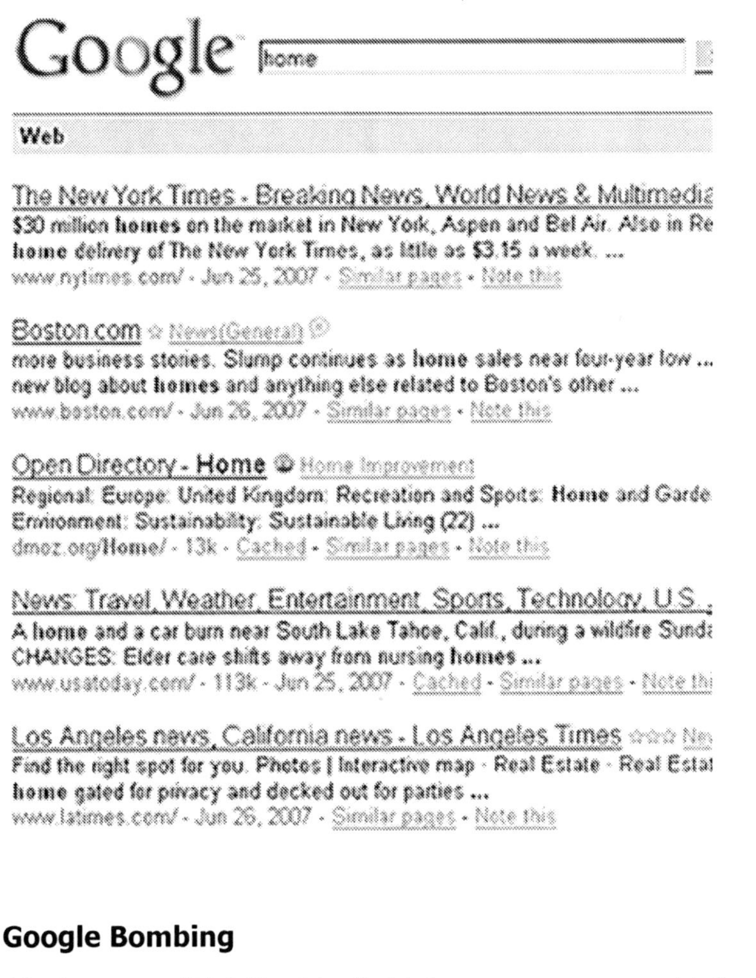

Google Bombing

Also known as "Link Bombing", this is a strategy to try and influence the ranking of a web page in Google's results based on link text manipulation. This strategy was primarily used by web sites with a humorous or political motive, which came to light when a search for "miserable failure" or "failure" brought up the Whitehouse's web site (whitehouse.gov/president) as the #1 result (basically a form of attack on President G.W. Bush). See screenshot[3] below.

Since then, Google has made its algorithms smarter to overcome such blatant trickery, but the basic concept still remains the same: Link Text is extremely important, and is valued highly on incoming links.

---

[3] Photo source: Flickr.com/photos/dannysullivan/369539947/

PageRank and Link Exchange Tips

PR is specific to a page, and not to a web site. For instance, your home page will almost always end up with a higher PR than the rest of the pages of your site. This is normal, since the home page is what most people will probably promote first, and the most, when exchanging links.

When exchanging links, if you are promoting your home page, then make sure your incoming link has just the domain name and not the file name of your home page. For ex., if your home page file name is `index.htm` or `index.html` or `index.php`, then don't specify the file name in the actual incoming link that you provide to your link exchange partners. They should be linking to http://www.Example.com

And *not* to any of the following:

http://www.Example.com/index.html
http://www.Example.com/index.htm
http://www.Example.com/index.php

The reason for this is the same as the previous point – that PageRank is specific to a page.

For instance, if you keep promoting links with an actual file name – like `Example.com/index.htm` - after a while, when you actually have PR for the above page, if you switch to a different file name - like `Example.com/index.php` - for any reason, and start promoting this new URL, then obviously, you will start getting incoming links to this new URL.

The bad news here is that Google considers the two links - `Example.com/index.htm and Example.com/index.php` as completely different from one another. So, the PR both versions will be different. This is why you need to leave out the actual index page's file name in your link exchanges and just point to your domain name.

Of course, if you are promoting a specific page on your web site – like `Example.com/car-buying-tips.html`, then of course, you will have to use the full file name in your link exchanges.

Deep Linking

Deep linking occurs when you get an incoming link to a page within (or *deep* inside, even if it is not so deep inside) your web site. In fact, deep linking is another important aspect factor in calculating PageRank.

Just because PageRank is page specific doesn't mean you should publish all forms of linkbait[4] directly on your home page, or just keep promoting your home page in all link exchanges.

It is OK if people link to an inner web page or blog post. If that page ends up getting more PageRank than your home page itself, it is still extremely beneficial to you, because you can then transfer PageRank from that inner page to any other page of your choice – which would obviously include your <wink>home page, of course</wink>.

So, if that high-PR-inner-page links to just your home page, then your home page's PR will get a tremendous boost when its PR is calculated.

Just remember that a huge increase in incoming links doesn't mean your PR will automatically go very high. In fact, if Google sees an overnight surge in your incoming links, then it might suspect that you are a spammer, and may put your site in the sandbox, or might even ban you from its index.

So, don't be scammed into purchasing software or services that promise you thousands of incoming links overnight. Also do not use software or services that claim to get you indexed in all the search engines within a few days, or even promise you "top page ranking" or claim to submit

---

[4] LinkBaiting is the strategy of getting other sites to link to your site by publishing something interesting; see section on linkbaiting in the chapter "Link Popularity")

you to hundreds of search engines or directories with the click of a button.

Using this kind of automatic, software-driven techniques can only get you into trouble with the search engines, especially with Google, and may even get your site banned, if not delay your site in getting indexed.

So use caution when building your web site, or its incoming links, and build high quality content and incoming links gradually, over time.

PageRank and Affiliate Links

It is possible that you have read that starting an affiliate program and having all those affiliate links that contain your domain name will increase your PageRank. This is only partially true. If you have hundreds of affiliate, each with a link that looks like:

`http://Example.com/aff/?id=Jack`

`http://Example.com/aff/?id=Jill`

.. and so on, remember that this will only increase the PageRank of the **aff** directory's index page (`index.htm` or `index.php`) – which means, the PageRank will go up for the url http://Example.com/aff/ and not the url of your home page, which is http://Example.com .

Now, if you think about it, there isn't much point to getting a high PR for your **aff** directory, because this page probably only contains information about your affiliate program, payout rate, terms and conditions. This page would never show up in a search for your actual keywords of your home page or for the keywords related to the product or service that you are selling.

Keep in mind that simply having all those URL's that contain your domain name (even though they don't necessarily point to your actual home page url) still plays a role in your site's PageRank, but there is no proof to suggest that it is anything but a minor factor.

So, the only way having an affiliate program is really going to benefit your incoming link popularity is to have your home page – preferably, an `index.php` or `index.jsp` script-driven page (and not a static `index.htm` or `index.html` page) – handle your incoming affiliate link.

So, your affiliate's links would look like: http://Example.com/?id=Jack

http://Example.com/?id=Jill

These url's are technically the same as:
http://Example.com/index.php?id=Jack and
http://Example.com/index.php?id=Jill

But as we saw before, it is better to leave out the file name part (`index.php`), and it would still be the same.

Google ignores any text after the "?", technically known as the "query string". So, for Google's purposes, which also means for PageRank purposes, Google seems both the following URL's http://Example.com/?id=Jack and http://Example.com/?id=Jill as pointing to your home page http://Example.com, in spite of the difference in some of the text after the "?" (one has the text "Jack" and the other "Jill")

Because Google ignores the query string while evaluating PageRank, the following two links…

http://Example.com/?id=Jack

http://Example.com/?id=Jill

…are both technically considered as *two*, distinct incoming links to your *home page* - because if you chop off the text after the "?" on both of the above links, what you are left with is the link to your home page:

http://Example.com/

So, the more affiliate links you can get pointing to your home page, means more link popularity for your home page.

You could write up some custom PHP code (or hire someone to write it for you) that captures the affiliate's id, and then redirects the visitor to your real affiliate program's page..

So, the incoming link comes to http://Example.com/?id=Jack first, and then you could use a software redirect to take the affiliate's id (in this case, "Jack") and pass it on to your affiliate program software, like this: http://Example.com/aff/?id=Jack

So, you have effectively killed two flies (because I don't like killing birds) in one swat: i) Your affiliate links still point to your main URL and not to the URL of a sub-directory, which means you will see a boost in your PR, while at the same time, and ii) You have given your affiliates a way to potentially earn a piece of your profits.

But also remember, like I mentioned previously, it's not really that bad for your affiliate program's home page to get a high PR, because if you don't put too many outgoing links on that page, and link just to your home page, you could slingshot the high PR over to your home page by just linking to your home page from that page.

But then again, the content of your affiliate home page may have no relevance to the content of your home page (or even the product itself), so, you may not really benefit at all from the linking.

So, the best thing to do is to ensure, if possible, that all your affiliate links are pointing directly to your home page, and not to a sub-directory.

When looking for link exchange partners, don't just focus on just those with a high PR. Even though there is a lot of proof that suggests that getting incoming links from a high PR site is better than a link from a low PR site, in the long run, it doesn't really matter if the linking page has high PR or not. This is because sometimes Google places more importance on the relevancy of the content and web site of the linker, than just the PR of the linking page.

So, if you have a choice of getting an incoming link from a high-PR, low-relevance page, versus a low-PR, high-relevance page, pick the latter. You just can't go wrong with that strategy, because not only will Google consider the link more relevant, but also visitors to that page will probably click through more to your site using that link, than from a link that is completely irrelevant to your site's theme or topic.

The Google "Supplemental Index"

Referred to earlier in this chapter as the "Google Sandbox", the supplemental index is a separate index (database) of web sites that do not show up during a regular Google search (main index).

To see if your site is in the supplemental index, do a Google search as follows:

```
site:www.your-domain.com
```

You can also use the cool tool at oy-oy.eu.

This parallel universe of Google search results usually contains a) sites that are about to be placed into the main index – like new sites that have been in the cooler and monitored for a while just to make sure no new site with hundreds of incoming links spams the search results, and b) sites that used to be in the main index, but are now about to be de-indexed – like sites that are about to be banned for various reasons we saw before.

There is no way of telling how long sites will remain in the supplemental index before they are either promoted to the main index, or before they completely drop out of even the supplemental index – which means no information about the site will be available about the site on Google (doing a `site:example.com` search will show up an empty results page).

If you build your site or launch an incoming-links campaign too aggressively, Google may put you in the supplemental index, or may simply ban your entire web site from the index altogether (both the *main* and the *supplemental* indices). This means that you will not only disappear from the main search results, but your site will also begin to furiously lose any PageRank it already has.

Many times, you can get blacklisted thus even if you are doing legitimate SEO, and are not doing anything sneaky or spammy (at least, not intentionally).

Because Google is so large and dominate the industry, it is next to impossible to get them to give you a reason as to why your site is not showing up in a Google search. At most, you may get a canned email from them referring you to a FAQ page that has details about getting your site indexed or un-black-listed.

If your site does get blacklisted, you will see that you can no longer find any information about your site in Google. All of the following will come up with no information:

```
info:Example.com
site:Example.com
link:Example.com
"Example.com"
```

Here are a few things that you can do to move from the supplemental index to the main index, or to get un-blacklisted:

Don't build a huge number of links overnight

This means, don't launch a big budget, incoming-link-building campaign in a very short period of time.

Even though it appears to make no sense, because popularizing a web site as fast as possible is every site owner's wish, doing too much too soon can make you look like spammers who use automated software to create and launch a large number of "supplemental" web sites overnight with a fraudulent link scheme that tries to trick search engines into thinking that this is a popular site, by building up a large number of fake incoming links.

No sneaky programming or keyword spamming

Do not use cloaked pages, auto-refresh pages, or any code (like JavaScript) you may have installed to manipulate your pages such that your visitors see one version, and the search engine robots see another.

Analyze your site to see if you are keyword spamming (repeating a keyword too many times just to obtain a higher ranking for that keyword), even if inadvertently, on any of your pages.

Try to reverse any recent changes you may have made that could potentially have been construed as spam by Google – like linking to questionable or spammy-looking sites while doing a link exchange.

Don't Overdo Cross-linking

Are you doing too much cross-linking between your various sites? Are you linking to or from your own web sites that may be irrelevant, or themselves may be considered spammy or questionable?

Avoid Duplicate Content

Don't create pages with very similar content with just a few tweaked keywords just for the sake of appearing higher up in the rankings. These are called "doorway pages" and Google is really good at detecting them and penalizing you for that. Completely avoid having sub-domains with similar content as your main web site. Similarly, do not host the same content on multiple hosts under different domain names just to build link popularity, by trying to point all of these duplicate sites to the main site. Those are sure-fire ways to get blacklisted.

If you create multiple, legitimate web sites with a similar theme to your main web site, then try to at least host them on a few different hosts, and not all on the same host which might end up with all sites having a very similar IP address (IP: Internet Protocol), which is again the signature of a spammer.

For better rankings, make sure your pages don't have the HTML editor assigned default title of "Untitled" or "Home" or just "Example.com" on all of your pages. Make every page have a distinct page title, and if possible unique description too.

Don't buy or publish "run of site" links (these are links where every page of a 3rd party web site – even if it's your own – links to your main site from each and every page on the third party web site.

You may even be doing this inadvertently. For example, you may have multiple sites on totally different topics, and in the navigation menu of each site, you may have links to each of your different sites.

Now, this may seem like a very natural thing to do – meaning, if you own five web sites, what is really the harm in publicizing your own web sites, right? I mean, if you don't link to your own web sites, how can you expect to others? This is similar to the "eat your own dog food" issue, you would think. However, Google may not necessarily feel the same. The search engine spider may conclude that you have just purchased links on a list of un-related web sites, and are "artificially" trying to influence your rankings in a search.

Technically speaking, SEO is truly nothing, but the art of artificially boosting rankings. However, when the motive behind SEO becomes questionable, then that's where you can start getting into trouble with the SE's (search engines).

Once again, what is *questionable* to you may not be questionable content to Google – and vice versa. So, tread the SEO path with utmost caution, and just remember that as long as you are building quality content for humans and building link relationships with quality web sites, and frequently updating your web site and actively notifying Google and other search engines and directories, you cannot really go wrong.

Other Tools, Tips and Tricks

Keyword Research

A major part of SEO is in knowing what the most popular keywords are that people are searching for, for a given topic. When you know what keywords people are searching for, then you can optimize your site's URL's, file names, title tag keywords, and the content on your pages for these keywords.

When there is a match between what people are looking for, and the content on your page, then assuming you have a high-enough PageRank, then you will show at the top of search results for a given search.

Keyword research is an integral part of optimizing your site. There are many tools available to do this, some for a fee, and some free. However, there isn't any *one* tool that you can totally rely on for accuracy, because each of these tools have their own limitations and algorithms, and the big search engines don't really give out too many details about the searches being performed, because the more information they give out, the more easy it becomes for spammers to reverse engineer the process and spam the engines and dominate the results with spammy, irrelevant sites.

So the best strategy is to use one or more of the following tools to arrive at your own internal conclusions and list of potential keywords that you need to optimize your site for.

SEO Elite - `seoelite.com`

Keyword Elite - `keywordelite.com`

IBP (Internet Business Promoter):
`axandra-web-site-promotion-software-tool.com`

OptiLink: `Windrosesoftware.com/optilink/`

Overture Keyword Tool: `inventory.overture.com`

This tool gives you all of the searches in the past month done at all of Yahoo's properties. On a generic level, you can expect the actual keywords being searched, and the number of searches for each of those keywords, to be quite similar between Yahoo and Google. So, you won't be too far off if you use this tool to optimize your site for Google as well.

Google Keyword Tool:

`Adwords.google.com/select/KeywordToolExternal:` This tool gives a fairly good estimate of the kind of searches and the traffic level for the keywords. This tool is primarily built for AdWords advertisers, so they can research various keywords, the number of searches they get, and optimize their pay-per-click advertising budgets.

WordTracker: `Wordtracker.com`

This is a commercial, non-free tool that is considered top-of-the-line for keywords research. This may be overkill for you if you are just starting out, but once you start making some money off of your web site, and wish to take your keyword research to the next level, this software is a must-have for your tool-kit.

WordPress Plugins and Customization

There are many add-ons (a.k.a. plugins) freely available for WordPress that can make you extremely productive, while allowing you to do customize your blog and add some *bling* to it. Here are some plugins I use myself, and highly recommend.

Google SiteMap Generator:
`arnebrachhold.de/2005/06/05/google-sitemaps-generator-v2-final`

This one allows you to create a specialized file in a special format (an XML file) as required by Google's "Sitemap" webmaster tool. With the click of a button, you can create this sitemap.xml file based on your blog posts, and the plug-in will also ping (notify) Google that there is a new version for download.

Adsense Plugin:
philhord.com/phord/adsense-inline-with-wordpress-blog-posts/

This plugin lets you add Adsense ads to your posts, simply by typing in a keyword, "<!—adsense-->" wherever you want the ad to show up.

Recent posts:
coffee2code.com/archives/2004/08/27/plugin-customizable-post-listings/

Display Recent Posts, Recently Commented Posts, Recently Modified Posts, Random Posts, and other post listings.

Math Comment Spam Protection
sw-guide.de/wordpress/plugins/math-comment-spam-protection/

Asks the visitor making the comment to answer a simple math question. This is intended to prove that the visitor is a human being and not a spam robot. Example of such question: *What is the sum of 2 and 9?*

Akismet
Akismet.com

Another spam-protection plugin. Free for personal use, about $5 per month for commercial use.

Spam Karma
Unknowngenius.com/blog/wordpress/spam-karma/

This is another spam-protection plugin.

WPZipper
wpzipper.com

Pick & choose the themes & plugins you want and get a WordPress install file with everything already installed

Customizing WordPress:

WordPress is one of the most exquisitely designed and developed open-source web applications available today. It is highly customizable and extensible, and the fact that it is open-source has resulted in a large community of contributors, who gladly write add-ons and plug-ins to the core application.

Plus because it is open-source and written in a very popular language (PHP), you can either customize it further by writing your own code, or you can easily hire an inexpensive developer who can do the coding for you.

The main look-and-feel (L&F) of all pages is controlled by *themes* and *templates*. There is a main "theme" that is made up of multiple templates like main template, single-page template, the CSS file that controls the styles, and so on.

After you've uploaded and enabled a theme, if you set the permissions for these files to be writable (CHMOD 777), then you can log in to your WordPress admin control panel and modify your current theme's templates right from your browser.

You can easily add and modify the content of each of these pages if you know a little bit of HTML and/or PHP. But even if you don't, you can always hire someone to do it for you for a very small expense, or you could try and barter your services in exchange for this work.

For more up-to-date info about Wordpress plugins and themes, visit `RaviRecommends.com`

7. Link Popularity

For long-term success in getting and maintaining high PageRank, building Link Popularity should be an integral part of your SEO strategy.

There are many ways in which you can get incoming links. Most of them require some work for sure, but some require more *creativity* than *hard work*. You have almost got to think like an ad agency that has been hired to generate publicity for you. Some ways are pleasant and creative, others are sneaky and dirty.

As long as you know the rules and play by the book, you can create a great number of incoming links to your site. The more links you want and the faster you want them, the more creative you need to be in your "PR" (in this case public relations) strategy.

Link Exchange: A Complete Waste of Time

I have to tell you the truth: The hunt for two-way links is mostly a big waste of time. No, not just *big*, but a *huge* waste of time.

In the beginning, it will be exciting to send out and receive emails about exchanging links with other web sites. It is all part of growing up (in e-Business). It's like the excitement you feel when you first buy your own house – in the beginning you want to do everything yourself, and so you go out and buy all kinds of expensive home and garden tools wanting to do everything yourself, and spend hours on mowing, weeding and seeding the lawn, taking care of the garden, shoveling the snow - only to ultimately end up getting tired of it all and outsourcing all (if not, most) of it.

Link Exchange will similarly tire you out eventually. You will realize that the amount of work you put into contacting webmasters of sites in your niche (or related niches) is incredibly disproportional to the number of valuable links that you end up getting.

It is almost like being at an MLM meeting: everyone who is attending such meetings is losing money, not making a single penny, yet they continue to do it just because someone has convinced them that they can be successful by cold-calling and embarrassing themselves and their friends and family and viewing everyone they meet as a "potential sucker".

You will quickly notice that all those approaching you for a link exchange are newbie site owners like you – most of whom have little or no PageRank, have a few hundred outgoing links to their "link partners", all from the same page (that has little or no PageRank either), link to all of your competitors too, effectively making the exchange totally worthless.

Okay, so maybe they are not totally worthless – but they are quite close. You get the point.

Yes, you can use software to automate these link exchange requests, but as you mature in your e-business, you will see that you yourself get many such spammy link exchange emails, and you begin to ignore almost all of them.

So, even though I think sending out link-exchange requests is a complete waste of your time, I will still describe all linking strategies for the sake of full topic coverage.

Link Exchange: Two-way Links

This is the most popular, but least effective way to get incoming links to your web site. Do a Google search for keywords related to your web site, make a list of the other sites that show up in the search results, contact the webmasters or site owners of each of these sites and ask them if they are willing to exchange links – you link to their site, and they link to yours.

Now, most large, professional sites will not link to your site when you are first starting out, and will probably ignore your request, more so because they have some PageRank and you probably don't. So, the exchange would be considered lop-sided (in your favor). But when you first launch your site, this can be an interesting way to learn how to contact other site owners, and to hone your PR and email skills, and probably even get a few incoming links along the way. Once again, this is part of growing up, like I mentioned before. So you should just do it and get it out of the way.

As you grow and have a product of your own, and your web site starts to look more professional, you will find it a lot easier to approach other site owners about exchanging links.

Especially, once your PageRank starts improving, and you get at least a PR of 2 or 3, you will find that more webmasters are willing to exchange links with you, just for the sake of your PR.

You should create a page called something like `links.html` where you publish the links of your link exchange partners, and similarly they would have such pages where they would publish your link.

It is recommended that you provide your partners with the exact HTML code, including the link, link-text and description, so that you are in control of the exact link text and URL that is pointing to your web site. If you don't provide them with the code, then they might create it randomly and the resulting incoming link or its link text may not be optimized enough to help your PR.

One-Way Links

Link exchange results in a two-way linking structure: You link to a site, and they link back to you. But Google incorporated a very smart rule – they said, if you are linking to a site and they are linking back to you, it is not a sign of the other site voluntarily linking to you because of your quality content, but a sign of the other site linking to you only because you returned the favor and linked back to them.

So sensibly (but unfortunately, for us site owners), Google discounts two-way links, and gives higher value to one-way links, where one site links to another site, but the second site has no links back to the first one.

One-way links carry more weight because they come across as a genuine "vote" from the linking web site to the "linkee" (site that is being linked to).

While any form of incoming links (even if they are two-way) are better and definitely help your PR than no links at all, in the overall scheme of things, it is better to try and focus on getting as many one-way links as possible, because that is what can truly send your PageRank skyrocketing, and in turn shoot up your ranking in the search results.

There are many ways to build one-way links, some of which are detailed below.

Ask specifically for One-Way Links

When you approach other webmasters for a link exchange, you should also try to find out if they are willing to give you a one-way link in return for some kind of an incentive – you could create a bonus product just for this, or you can purchase resell rights to a digital product online. Here's an email I send out asking for a link exchange:

```
Hi <site owner's name/webmaster>,

My name is Ravi Jayagopal and I'm the owner of
BabyNamesIndia.com .

I wanted to email about a possible partnership
opportunity.

1. May I offer you software that I have developed
myself, at http://www.WebmasterInABox.net and
http://www.VirtualTypingAssistant.com in return for a
one-way link from your home page to my site
http://www.BabyNamesIndia.com ?

2. If you won't accept software, then how much would
you charge me for a one-way link from your home page?

3. I have an affiliate program at:
http://www.BabyNamesIndia.com/affiliates.html where
you can make up to $12 per sale of our ebook, simply
recommending our ebook using a special "affiliate
```

```
link". I use ClickBank for the sales, which you may
have heard of. So check out the above link.

If there is any other way that our sites can partner
for mutual benefit, do let me know as I'm certainly
open to ideas.

Look forward to your response.

Thanks,

Ravi

http://www.BabyNamesIndia.com
```

Most people opt for the link exchange, but because I asked them the question about one-way links, I have had about 20% of the site owners replying that they wouldn't mind the software/one-way link barter, and I have ended up with some pretty decent one-way links from this kind of a deal.

And also because I gave them multiple options, than just saying "exchange links with me", they end up choosing one or the other, and in many cases write back to me asking about my affiliate program.

And my affiliate program links are carefully and deliberately designed such that they increase my PageRank. So, when affiliates link to my site using their special affiliate link, they are doing so using my domain name in the affiliate link, which also ends up helping my PageRank.

Read more about this in "PageRank and Affiliate Links" further ahead.

Multi-way Links

This is part of the "Mini Network" strategy explained further below. But the main idea is something like this:

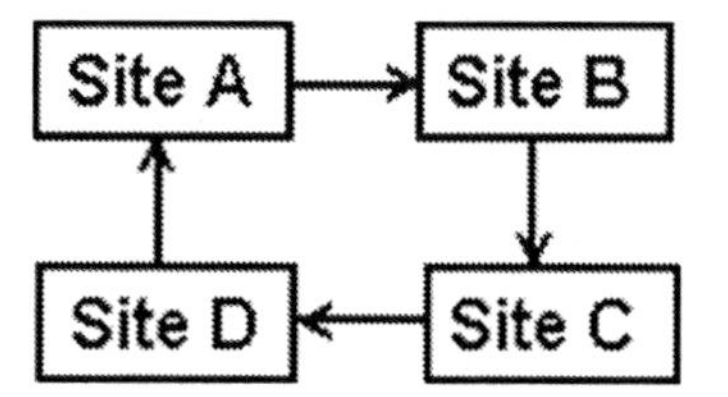

If you notice, none of the sites link back to the linker (the site linking to them). They are all one way links, and finally the last site (Site D) in the chain links back to the first one. I'm pretty sure Google has ways of detecting this, but this kind of a set up is still much better at passing on PageRank than a typical link exchange, which reeks of link manipulation.

The key here is that if you owned Sites B, C and D yourself, you can control the "link love" (PageRank) distribution a lot more effectively than you could if someone else owned those sites.

Mini-Networks

There are various mini-network strategies. Many of them are spammy strategies and involve gray-hat techniques, so we won't go there in this book.

The white-hat, fully legitimate way to use a mini-network for increasing PageRank, is to basically create a number of separate, fully functional, fully independent web sites that are closely related to the theme of your main (money making) site. See the image below.

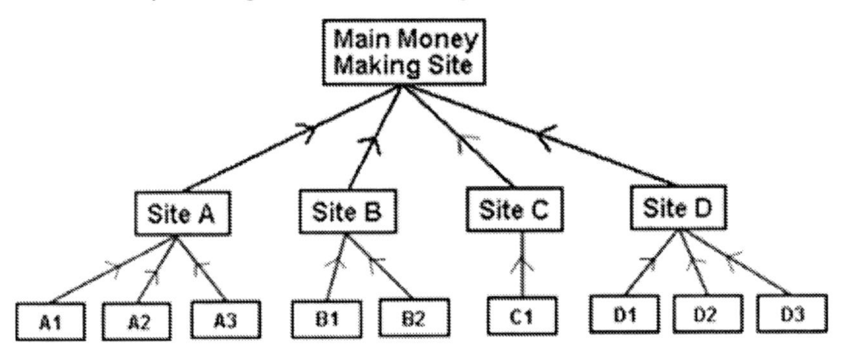

The image shows a sample network of sites, all working together to increase the PageRank of the main site.

The usual way to build incoming links is to contact various sites (like Site A, Site B, Site C and Site D) belonging to others, that are closely related to your niche, and ask them for one-way links or buy one-way links from them, like we saw in a previous section. Now obviously, these external sites (Sites A, B, C and D) are going to have other incoming links from other external, 3rd-party owned sites like A1, A2, B1, C1, etc. And in turn they will be linking to other web sites like your main web site.

Now the mini-network strategy is very similar to the usual way explained above. The only difference is that instead of contacting the site owners of high-ranking 3rd-party sites like Site A and B, you yourself would create such sites with the long term in mind, with the primary goal of passing on the PageRank to your main site.

When those external sites belong to others, it is hard to convince them to give you one-way links. It is also hard to get them to link to you the way you want, from the pages you want, using the link-text you want. You could fast track this process by paying a price for those links, but even when you do so, there will be other outgoing links on that site which will dilute the PageRank influence from those pages.

The location and types of links and the distribution of PageRank, is something you cannot control on other people's web sites.

But imagine if you owned all of those sites. Now how easy would it be to make sure that you are passing PageRank only to sites you own - or to sites that are important to you – like sites of clients, friends, business associates, etc?

Yes, developing a number of other web sites that are closely related to your own site takes a lot of time and effort. In fact, you will initially be so busy building your main web site that you should not be focusing on building these other sites.

That is why this is considered an advanced strategy for those who have built up their main site to some extent, and are now moving to the next level of increasing PageRank to a new high, and competing with the next level of competitors.

However, keeping Google's sandbox in mind, it is not a bad idea to register the domain names now, and to at the least, create a quick web site (maybe slap on a WordPress blog at the domain) and let the web site and domain name gain age and authority (something that Google loves!)

Don't develop these sites much to start with – maybe you can just post a few articles or posts based on content you have already created, and then use Blog-and-Ping and Blog-and-Bookmark to get the url's of these sites out there, so that over a period of time, they will start to show some minimal PageRank.

During this time, you would have been building and marketing your main site. There will come a time when you need to start focusing heavily on SEO to get to the next level. That's when you start pulling up these sites one by one, and start developing them as independent web sites.

Now, if you have the budget, you can pay folks like yours truly, who offer SEO services, or hire consultants from sites like RentACoder.com or Workaholics4Hire.com to build these sites in parallel as you build your main site, so your entire network slowly expands over time.

PageRank of Leaf Nodes

Over a period of time, as you build your network, you will end up with a number of Leaf Nodes (like Sites A1, A2, B1, etc) – the bottom most sites that are linking up but don't have too many incoming links themselves.

You will have to work on a link-popularity strategy for these sites, using other techniques described in this chapter, so that these leaf nodes also get some PageRank over time. Without these nodes having PageRank, the rest of the network will be rendered useless. The primary goal is to increase the PageRank of the main site, and for this to work, the PageRank of the entire mini-network has to be worked on concurrently.

LinkBait

If you genuinely build a web site with usable content and keep updating it with quality content, you can get a lot of people to voluntarily link to you, without you even asking for them. There are a number of small mom-and-pop web sites out there that are nothing more than a directory of links to web sites in a variety of niches. These rarely-maintained "hobby" web sites manage to get a decent PageRank over time, and one-way links from a number of such sites can prove to be a huge factor in increasing your own PageRank.

LinkBaiting is just an extension of building something worthy, and is the act of deliberately and tactfully creating something interesting, new, educational, viral, outrageous or controversial - so that others can talk about you and link to your site. The ultimate goal is to get incoming links, period.

This is quite similar to "viral marketing", except that in viral marketing, the main goal is getting free traffic to your product or service that you are promoting, to improve brand recognition, increase leads or improve sales.

Getting traffic and getting links are two completely different things. Getting a lot of incoming links may not result in a lot of traffic, but will certainly result in higher PageRank. And similarly, getting a lot of traffic will not necessarily result in your site getting many one-way links, because traffic generation can be done in multiple ways, some of them in non-web ways (like news items in newspapers, radio and TV).

If you think about it, linkbait is the only way you should be building web sites.

In the old Pre-PageRank days, everyone who was building content online was building it so that others would find it interesting, exciting, educational, funny or even outrageous. That's how the real web was built – full of great content (all those newbie pages on Geocities.com and Tripod.com with flashing images and Java applets notwithstanding) and people linking to others' web sites only to give their visitors more choices and more information. The real web didn't worry about incoming links or outgoing links, and links were genuinely used as a "vote of confidence" for another web site. The real web did not worry about using "nofollow" links or links generated with JavaScript or cloaked links encoded in Flash.

Somewhere along the way, Google came along and said, the more incoming links you have, the higher you will show up on our web site. They gave us a scoreboard called PageRank, and asked us to go knock each other out trying to compete!

Somewhere along the way, the web became more about writing content just to get incoming links and show up higher for more keywords by including all kinds of researched keywords into one's copy rather than writing from the heart.

Oh, how the web has changed! But guess what, one has got to adapt. The good news is that the old-school of creating quality content is still amongst the most popular of strategies, especially when it comes to getting incoming links.

Creating content worthy of being linked to by others is currently the most powerful way of getting a large number of one-way links.

Viral marketing uses a variety of techniques – like incentives in the form of points, money, free gifts or bonuses, some form of affiliate promotion, or just the sheer joy of being the first to telling someone about your web site – in order to bring a lot of traffic to your web site. This may or may not result in many people linking to you, because a lot of it could happen via email and/or word-of-mouth.

But linkbaiting very specifically targets getting more incoming links from other web sites to improve PageRank. After all, isn't that what the web was built for, for people to link to other sites and pages of their choice, and to "spread the word"?

So, even though the concept of linkbaiting – which is creating something worthy of mention, something worth talking about, worth linking to – is a very old concept, and very common in the off-line world, the strategy received a formal title in the web world only in the recent past.

There are numerous ways to create linkbait:

- Publish hard-to-find news or information
- Expert opinion or review of a product, service or web site
- Something to entertain or educate
- Something exciting, controversial, outrageous
- A picture or video
- A free, online service or tool

- Downloadable content (e.g., a report or software)

The old model of gaining subscribers to your newsletter, or basically get leads for your business - was to promise to give people some kind of special information, *if* they give you their email addresses *first*.

This special information could be access to some useful information you have found, access to a report or a free download or a tool.

But in the last couple of years, so called "Internet marketers" have abused this "subscribe first, get access later" model so much, that it now just infuriates people when you ask them for their email address first.

In fact, I must've subscribed from at least a few hundred lists in the last one year, because all of these Internet pimps get your email address under the pretext of some "exclusive report", and once the weak, watered down, "exclusive report" or tool has been delivered, all they do is bombard you with affiliate promotions for high-priced items.

The whole Internet marketing model is changing. The trend is slowly changing from a spammy "mailing list" model to a infinitely more powerful opt-in model: RSS-Feed Subscription. In this model, your visitors have the choice of subscribing to your feed to their feed reader (like the web-based one at LinkOverLoad.com) if they think your content is worthy of their eyeballs and time.

They now have the ability to consume your feed when they want, how they want, *if* they want.

During such a hyper-sensitive time when people are shying away from anyone who asks for their email address, much like the total stranger who asks you for your phone number at a bar, it is extremely important that you offer something first before you ask your visitors for something in return.

The only way to be really successful today, is to simply open-up access to all of your information. No more hiding information. Display it all on your web site, on your blog, on your feeds. And then ask people boldly for their subscription. If what you have to offer is any good, you will get them to stay, and come back too.

Authority Sites

One way to get listed quickly on Google, and getting more weight for your incoming links, is to get those links from *Authority Sites,* which basically are popular sites with lots of traffic, and for many reasons, have earned Google's trust.

Of course, Google has ways of dealing with and weeding out link-spam even from such authority sites. For example, Wikipedia (the web's foremost community-built encyclopedia) has always been considered among the top authority sites. But unfortunately, where there is a system, there are always going to be folks who abuse the system.

The link-spam on Wikipedia got so bad, that eventually Wikipedia marked all external links using the "rel=nofollow". However, this is an ongoing discussion that you can follow by visiting:

`http://en.wikipedia.org/wiki/Wikipedia:Nofollow`

Some of the authority sites that Google seems to trust are:

Squidoo.com: This is a site founded by Seth Godin, the godfather of business blogging.

Digg.com/Reddit.com/Del.icio.us/Netscape: These are among the more popular community sites, and while all of them can bring you a tremendous amount of traffic (especially if you can get to the main page) the links from Netscape are the ones which usually seem to show up the highest in Google's search results.

Article Sites: EzineArticles.com is the biggest player, followed by others like GoArticles.com and ArticleCity.com. See next section about writing articles.

Classifieds Services: Posting ads and messages on sites like `CraigsList.org`, `Answers.Yahoo.com` and `USFreeAds.com`.

Blog Services: You could create mini-sites (or mini-blogs) with content related to your primary web site, on sites like Squidoo.com, WordPress.com, Blogger.com and GooglePages.

PRWeb.com: This is another authority site that Google loves. You can not only use them for press releases, but you can also use the trackback feature on their site to send *them* trackbacks from *your* blog when you write about and refer to a press release on their site (even if it is not your own release), which means you can get a free link back from their site.

There are times when I'm hunting for content for some of my niche sites, and I head over to PRWeb.com to look for interesting press releases. In the beginning, I just used to copy-paste the release from their web site to my site, but later on I released that you can also send a trackback to the page that lists the press release, and get back a one-way link from them.

An incoming link from an authority site like PRWeb only means more link-love for your site.

YouTube.com: Yes, YouTube! Ever since Google unified its search results (relevant results from its web index, images, maps, news and video all showing up together), more and more video results are showing up in their results pages. Which means a video on YouTube that has your keywords in the video's title (like "how to throw your voice") will show up as a thumbnail in searches for the same keywords (Try this: `Google.com/search?q=how+to+throw+your+voice`).

How to Find Authority Sites

Do a Google search for just about any set of keywords – maybe start with keywords that you have identified for your own web site.

Then, browse through the various web sites showing up on the results pages, and try to identify links from major information portals (like Wikipedia.org, About.com, Yahoo.com), social networking sites (Digg, Netscape and yes, even YouTube), classifieds sites (Ebay.com, CraigsList.com), community sites (SlashDot.com, Webmaster forums, Google and Yahoo groups, YouTube.com), News sites (CNN.com, Google News, PR Web) and article repositories (EzineArticles.com, GoArticles.com).

Make a list of the authority sites you found in the search results. Remember, the kind of authority sites that show up in the results will differ from niche to niche: Webmasterworld.com and SlashDot.org are authority sites when it comes to the techie world, but links from them to your site on Pregnancy and Parenting may not carry much weight at Google. So, you have to find the *relevant* authority sites for your niche.

The next thing to do is to get an incoming link from such sites.

Submitting Content to Authority Sites

Sites like About.com and EzineArticles.com will allow you to upload articles, classifieds sites will let you add ad postings, sites like PRWeb will accept news releases, and other community sites like SlashDot will allow you to make forum postings.

Find out what kind of content is acceptable to each of the authority sites identified earlier, and make sure you add relevant content with the right keywords, linking to the right pages on your web site (not all links have to point to your home page).

Sites like Dmoz.org carry huge weight when it comes to Google and Yahoo. In fact, Yahoo and MSN use Dmoz listings in their search results to show your title and description. But it is not easy to get into the Dmoz directory, as it is maintained by humans, and they are very low on resources.

In fact, when you first apply for Dmoz inclusion of your web site, thoroughly check the information you are submitting for not just accuracy, but also to make sure that they have the right keywords in the right places, and a proper description that will not only help you rise in the SERP's, but will also help you get more clicks. Once you submit your information and if/when it does eventually appear on Dmoz, it is next to impossible to get it modified, because you simply won't get any response from the Dmoz folks, even if you go through the proper channel of making changes to your existing listing.

You could try to become an editor at Dmoz – not to cheat the system and add your own links, but to help out the extremely shorthanded community and help maintain sites in your (or other) niche.

Buying links on Authority Sites

Buying links on authority sites is the fastest way to get one-way links. You can try directly contacting the site owner or blogger through the contact-us form on their site or blog, or you can use ad-networks like `Text-link-ads.com` and `Adbrite.com`, who simplify the process of buying text links from a pool of web sites. They have signed up various publishers, who are categorized according to their topic, and you can bid or purchase ads from these networks, who in turn take a percentage of the sale as commission, before passing on the rest to the publishers themselves.

The Down Side of Buying Links

Buying links is a good short-term strategy for instantly seeing some traffic, especially if yours is a new site, and also when buying a link on a high-traffic web site may be far cheaper than buying PPC ads (say, on Google).

But paid text links are certainly not a good long term strategy for gaining PageRank, because the moment you stop running your ad, those sites will drop you from their site, which means you lose the PageRank they were passing on to you. So, once your ad is dropped from a site, it is only a matter of time before you see a drop in PageRank as well.

If you can pull of low-cost links on low-profile web sites, and keep a sufficient budget for long-term advertising, then buying links can give your PR a huge boost.

You can also try to sponsor local and non-profit web sites, who may give you a one-way link in return for your sponsorship.

The other issue with buying links through sites like Text-link-ads.com is that Google is continuously getting smarter at detecting the "intention" behind incoming links to your site. Obviously, there is no way of finding out exactly what parameters they use in determining whether an incoming link is an "influenced" link (link exchange or paid links), but we certainly do know that Google does discount such influenced links, and gives more weight to "editorial" type links (links from a review on another site, recommendation links, and links in blogs).

Even with blogs, there are sites like PayPerPost.com which will allow you to pay bloggers to write an original review about your product or service, but because of the disclaimer that they have to include within the post itself (that the said post has been sponsored), it is very easy for even us readers, let alone Google, to figure out that those are not natural referral links. So obviously, you are not going to get much link juice from such paid-for links.

Even links from article exchanges are slowly losing weight, as Google figures out that those have an ulterior motive too (content exchange: you give the people who are publishing your articles free content, and in return they are linking back to you) and are not natural links.

As Google's quest for weeding out artificially influenced links continues, they will eventually figure out (along with some unfortunate false positives, of course) which are natural, "un-influenced", legitimate incoming links, and which ones aren't.

But regardless of how much it discounts links from certain sites, and regardless of whether your site's PageRank improves because of those links or not, following the authority-site model and gaining all those additional incoming links can only be good for your site, as it improves the exposure to your web site, which in turn will result in more traffic. More traffic, with very few exceptions, is always good, as it can lead to other good things – like more leads, conversions and eventually sales.

Write Articles

This is one of the foremost techniques in getting free incoming links from other web sites. Write a professionally worded, informational, educational or entertaining article about a topic in your niche, and submit it to the many article directories online.

Web site publishers always need content to publish, and keep looking for professional content. When you submit to the article directories, these publishers will pick up your article, and if you publish a good article, you can easily expect hundreds, if not thousands, or back-links from other sites within a few months.

There is software available to automate the submission of articles to a large number of directories.

As mentioned in an earlier chapter, the more popular article directories are EzineArticles.com, ArticleCity.com and GoArticles.com.

Submit Press Releases

Press releases are a great way to get some incoming links from some unusual resources, like news or information-based sites. Also, a press release can get you a different kind of publicity that is not possible simply link-baiting or viral marketing.

Participate in Online Discussions

You can get some quality free traffic by hanging out at hot-spots where your potential audience is hanging out too – like registering for bulletin boards and user forums at sites closely related to your site's theme, posting useful tips and messages, generally participating in ongoing discussions, and using your signature to link back to your site.

If a forum doesn't allow a signature or links in your signature, just move on to the next one - such forums are not worth your time, unless it is one where you are trying to establish yourself as an expert in your industry, and branding is more important than back-links.

For example, branding guru Rob Frankel has a forum called "Frankelbiz" (`Frankelbiz.com`) where one is not allowed to post signatures at the end of your emails. The only time you can publish your link is during an *intro* post where you introduce yourself and your business. But since this is a large, powerful community with serious business people – both people wanting to buy services, and people offering those services – this list is the place just to get serious business done. So, the list members do not mind the fact that you cannot add your web site link to the end of your post.

Commenting on Blogs

Posting comments on other people's blogs and guest-books (though guest-books are now considered a lot less important these days) and similarly using your signature to get a back-link. As comment-spam is increasing, blog owners are increasingly turning off the commenting feature. If that is the case, you can still get some link-love through Trackbacks (next topic).

Trackbacks on Blogs

Post a track-back from your blog to a post on someone else's blog – a post that has high PR or is relevant to your site's theme.

A *Trackback* occurs when you blog about someone else's blog posting, and send a "notification" from your blog software to the referred post's blog software, notifying that you have posted something that refers to or extends the main blog's post.

This notification, if approved by the blog owner, will then appear as a *trackback* entry in the *comments and trackbacks* section of that post, and this entry will also contain a link to your actual post where you made a reference to the main blog. So, you indirectly get a back-link to your blog.

8. SEO Case Study

HowToThrowYourVoice.com

I am an amateur ventriloquist. I got into it while trying to figure out ways to keep my daughter's friends entertained at one of her birthday parties. Long story short, I decided to create a web site to show off my vent skills, and make money off of ads while doing so, and maybe even make a digital product out of it.

So, one day I went and looked to see if there was any traffic for keywords like "ventriloquism", "how to throw your voice" and "puppets".

how to throw your voice
ventriloquist
ventriloquist dummy
ventriloquist dummies
ventriloquist dolls
ventriloquist doll
puppet
character puppet
hand puppet
puppet show
string puppet
finger puppet
sunny puppet

For this, I used the Google Keyword Tool at https://adwords.google.com/select/KeywordToolExternal , and to my surprise I found that there was an encouraging amount of searches for those keywords.

So, I registered the domain name `HowToThrowYourVoice.com` – which again, to my surprise, was still available. I created a hosting account on Dream-Host.biz (once you have one multi-site hosting account, adding a new site takes only a few minutes).

I quickly threw up a Wordpress blog on it, and wrote an introductory post. The whole cycle - from registering the domain name, creating a web hosting account, pointing my domain name to my new web site, installing Wordpress, *and* publishing my first post – took under 30 minutes.

In the next two months, I made just two more posts to the blog, and then completely forgot about it for a while, as I moved on to other more important projects (like finishing this book).

I keep smaller projects like this on the backburner all the time, and whenever I need a break from working on my main web sites or my other main projects, I pick up one of these little mini-projects and work on it till I get my energy level back up. Doing this keeps me from getting burned out, while also helping me develop these mini-projects slowly over time, which has its own advantages, as you'll see.

So, after having done absolutely nothing with the site for another 3 months, one day I got into another "mini-project zone" and updated the site with a few more posts, including the addition of some funny videos that I'd created, as well as some YouTube videos from some famous ventriloquists.

I added this site (the blog is my main site) to my FeedBurner.com account, so that I could track statistics like visitors to my posts, subscriptions to my feed and referrer URL's (where they are coming from).

Then, as I normally do with all of my new web sites, I sent out a "friendly spam" mail on June 16, 2007 to some of my close friends and relatives (the ones who seem to have a greater tolerance level for the "stuff" that I send them).

Screenshot of my "Sent" folder on Yahoo! Mail

ogroups.com	My new site about Ventriloquism: HowToThrowYourVoice.com	Sat Jun 16,
	My new site: HowToThrowYourVoice.com	Sat Jun 16,
	My new site: HowToThrowYourVoice.com	Sat Jun 16,
	Re: My new site: HowToThrowYourVoice.com	Sun Jun 17,
	Re: My new site: HowToThrowYourVoice.com	Sun Jun 17,
	Re: My new site: HowToThrowYourVoice.com	Mon Jun 18,
	Re: My new site: HowToThrowYourVoice.com	Mon Jun 18,

I also submitted one of the really funny posts - a video from YouTube (published on my blog using their "embed" code), featuring famous ventriloquist Jeff Dunham – to 3 of the popular social-bookmarking sites: Digg.com, Reddit.com and Netscape.com.

Because I wasn't really ready to start promoting the site, I didn't even bother submitting my blog to other such sites like Technorati.com and StumbleUpon.

Two days later, this (see screenshot below) is how my FeedBurner stats looked (I had some 20+ visitors on June 17th, and 44 visitors on the 18th).

FeedBurner Statistics

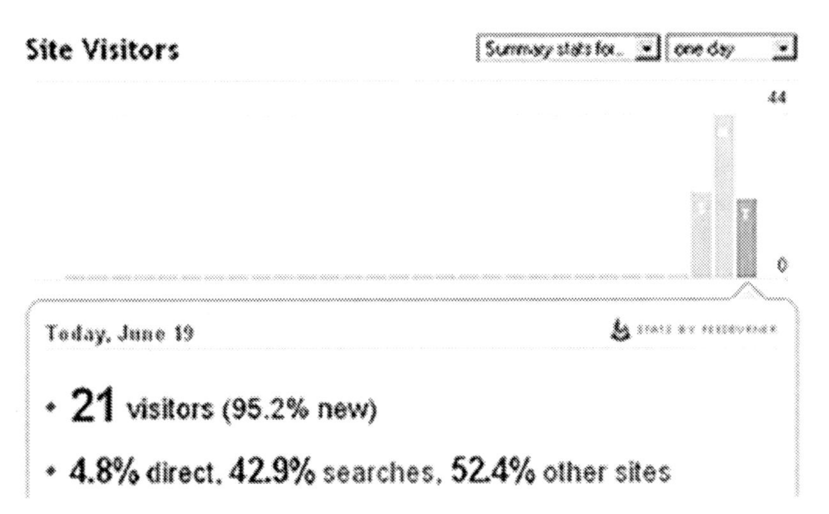

It was then I noticed that 42.9% of my visitors had come from "searches" and 52.4% from "other sites". Upon further investigation, the stats showed me that I was getting visitors from both Google and Yahoo for "how to throw your voice", among other keywords.

So, I quickly did a Google and Yahoo search for those keywords, and was absolutely blown away that not only had my site already gotten indexed by these search engines, but my site was actually showing up at position #3 on Yahoo – and #11 on Google (the first link on the 2nd page of results, as per my personal Google search setting of 10 results per page).

Yahoo Search Results for "How to throw your voice"

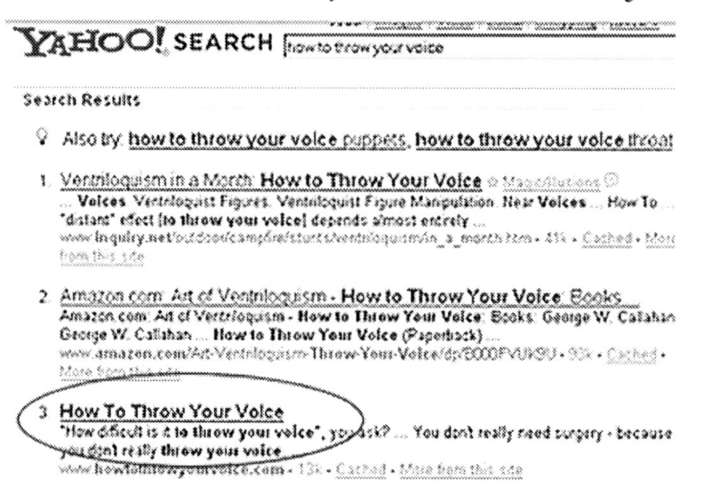

Note that up to this point, I had not done any search engine optimization whatsoever - I had not "submitted" my site to any search engine, I had not exchanged links with any site, I had not linked to it even from any of my own sites, I had not promoted it to my business lists, had not done any advertising or purchased links on any site. Heck, I didn't even have any PageRank, but I was showing up higher than sites that had PageRank 3, 4 and even 5!

All I had basically done was written 3 blog posts and submitted my site to 3 social-bookmarking sites just 2 days earlier.

Google search results for "How to throw your voice"

Google how to throw your voice

Web Results 11 - 20 of about 2,870,000 for how to throw your voice. (0.1

How To Throw Your Voice » Jeff Dunham and Walter: Arguing With Myself Humor
Please note: Comment moderation is enabled and may delay your comment ... David Strassman (4); How To Throw Your Voice (4); Jeff Dunham (1) ...
www.howtothrowyourvoice.com/2007/06/16/jeff-dunham-and-walter-arguing-with-myself/ - 14k - Jun 18, 2007 -
Cached - Similar pages - Note this

siouxlandlib.org: Throw Your Voice at Siouxland Libraries - 2:26pm
Throw Your Voice, a free ventriloquism workshop for teens, will be held at th Ronning Branch of Siouxland Libraries on Thursday, June 22, 2006, at 7 p.m.
www.siouxlandlib.org/teens/News/2006/June/throw_your_voice.aspx - 15k -
Cached - Similar pages - Note this

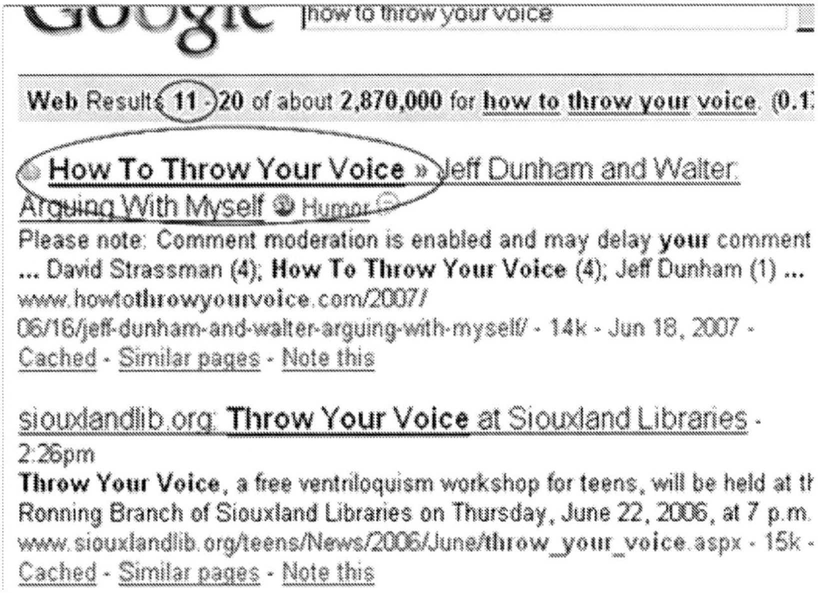

As I started investigating Google's search results further, I saw that my site was also listed on the *very first page* too, at position #9 (see the following screenshot).

But it was not a direct link to my web site, but instead a link to my article posted on Netscape, and the article in turn led to my web site.

So, even though it was not a direct link, I was still getting all the traffic, because anyone who followed that link to my Netscape article, also clicked through to my site through the article's main link.

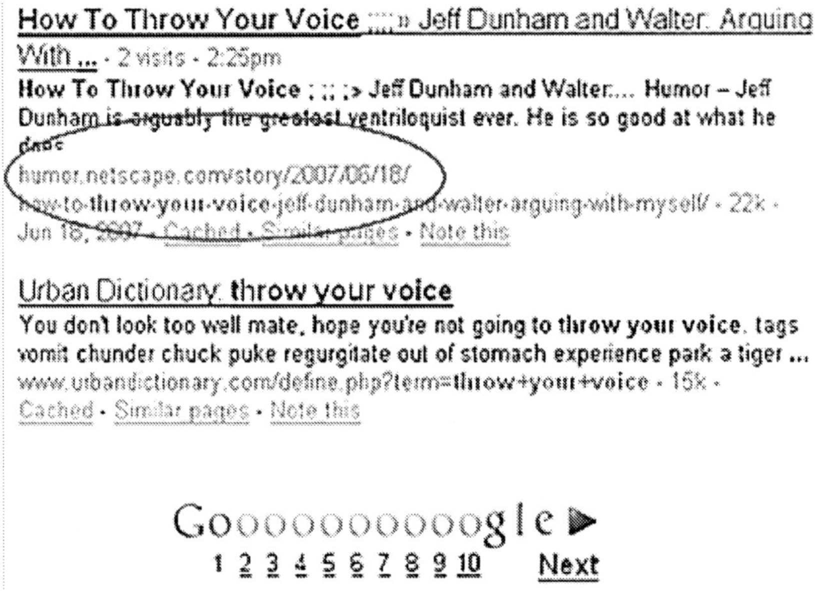

How To Throw Your Voice ;;;;» Jeff Dunham and Walter: Arguing With ... - 2 visits - 2:25pm
How To Throw Your Voice ; ;; ;» Jeff Dunham and Walter.... Humor – Jeff Dunham is arguably the greatest ventriloquist ever. He is so good at what he does
humor.netscape.com/story/2007/06/18/how-to-throw-your-voice-jeff-dunham-and-walter-arguing-with-myself/ - 22k - Jun 18, 2007 - Cached - Similar pages - Note this

Urban Dictionary: throw your voice
You don't look too well mate, hope you're not going to throw your voice. tags vomit chunder chuck puke regurgitate out of stomach experience park a tiger ...
www.urbandictionary.com/define.php?term=throw+your+voice - 15k - Cached - Similar pages - Note this

Gooooooooooogle ▶
1 2 3 4 5 6 7 8 9 10 Next

So the Netscape.com link, due to Netscape apparently being considered an "authority site", had gotten picked up and was showing up on ahead of many of the other 2.8 million web sites, all within just 2 days of my posting the link on Netscape.

Now *that* is the power of incoming links from authority sites.

As I write this chapter, about 2 weeks after I first took those screenshots, my site is #1 on Yahoo, and I have **not just one, but four first page listings** and **1 second page listing** on Google - #3 and #4 are direct links to my site, while #9 and #10 are indirect links to my site (one through Netscape.com, and the other through an question I cleverly answered at Yahoo! Answers (answers.yahoo.com).

Two of the 1st page listings on Google

Next two 1st page listings on Google

How To Throw Your Voice :» How To Be A Ventriloquist With
Even ...
How To Throw Your Voice: Jeff Dunham and Achmed the Dead... Humor -
is why Jeff Dunham is so great at this stuff. This following clip is insanely fun
humor.netscape.com/.../23/
how-to-throw-your-voice-how-to-be-a-ventriloquist-without-even-trying-to-bei
- 26k - Cached - Similar pages - Note this

Yahoo! Answers - How do you throw your voice?
You can't really throw your voice to "make it sound like you are across the
room". The term "throw your voice" is just a phrase for making it appear th
...
answers.yahoo.com/question/index?qid=20070623161738AAP4Qdi - 39k -
Cached - Similar pages - Note this

Gooooooooooogle ▶
1 2 3 4 5 6 7 8 9 10 Next

One 2nd Page "indirect" listing on Google:

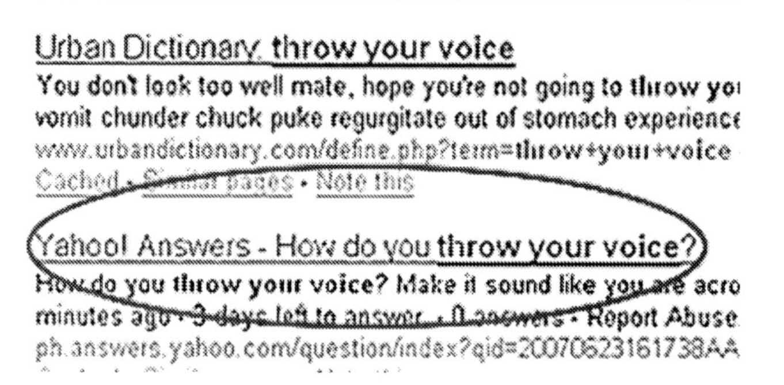

Before I took these screenshots, I had gone on to submit my sites to other social-bookmarking sites like `StumbleUpon.com`, `Furl.net` and `OnlyWire.com` (which lets me submit to several social-bookmarking sites together, by filling out just one form).

So, with Zero PageRank, absolutely no incoming links from any web site (not even my own) except of course from the social-bookmarking sites, with no link exchanges, no advertising, no link buying, my site came to #1 on Yahoo, #3 on Google, and got a total of 4 first-page listings and 1 second-page listing on Google.

So How The Heck Did This Happen?

It is very simple: Quite a few things actually came together, none of which are difficult to do, nor do they cost a cent.

Here are the major factors that I believe to have made this happen:

- **The power of Keywords**: The keywords that were being searched on, were either in my web page's content or in the URL (sometimes just the domain name, other times in the title of my post)
- **The power of Wordpress**: The titles of my posts were automatically included in the post's URL by Wordpress, which

as I mentioned before, is an extremely search-engine friendly strategy, which not only helps the search engines rank my posts, but also is a strong incentive for humans to click on, when the title is not a cryptic one, but a more descriptive one, like: `http://www.howtothrowyourvoice.com/how-to-talk-without-moving-your-lips/`

- **The power of Pinging**: Full credit to the blog-and-ping (with the right ping list, of course), tag-and-ping, and blog-and-bookmark strategies described earlier, which you saw in use here.

At the time of writing this chapter, HowToThrowYourVoice.com is averaging about 80 visitors a day (and I still haven't linked to it from any of my own web sites ☺).

9. Planning a Web Site

Why do you need a web site?

I mean, where is the need for a web site if you run a local hair salon and your customers don't live more than 5 miles away? Why would anyone visit the web site of the hair salon 'round the street corner? It's not like you can get a hair cut online, right? Wrong!

A web site is not just for selling stuff online. Think of a web site as an extension of your business - an extension of your self, an extension of your vision, your thoughts, emotions, hobbies, passion and ideas.

A web site's purpose is not always just to lead to instant revenue.

A web site could be used to generate leads for your offline business; used as a marketing tool to create new customers as well as bring back old customers. Use it to distribute information about your products and services that would normally require your customers to call you and wasting precious time in calling you, in waiting time, and in information exchange.

How about making the information available on-demand? After all, nothing is more important to your customers than to have all their questions answered right away - at any time of the day, or night. Put the power of information gathering at their fingertips - let them decide what they want to know, and when they want to know. Don't slow them down by making them jump through hoops like automated answering services or human representatives who probably know as much about your business as your customers.

If I were the hair salon owner, these are just a few things I would do with my web site to enhance my "local" business:

I would collect email addresses from customers - I would invite them to sign up for my newsletter so that I can send them discount coupons for their next visit by email. Not a bad incentive to get their attention and their email address. In fact, I would even go a step further, and have a computer right there at the cash counter, and have them enter their email address right there on my web site, right in front of me, so that I could print out the $5 discount coupon for their next visit right there on my printer in the store.

I would send them hair styling and coloring and hair care tips by email.

How about celebrity gossip? "Bad hair day" pictures of local or national celebrities? Or links to third-party web sites with interesting "hairy" stories?

How about interesting stories about incidents at the salon? I would keep a digital camera handy at the store, and take "Before" and "After" pictures of some really good styles, with the permission of the customer - after bribing them with a instantly redeemable, free, relaxing head and scalp massage offer, of course.

I would have an online appointment booking system, where they can reserve a slot ahead of time.

I would have a "Refer a Friend" program - the customer would get $5 off if their friend came to the salon for a hair cut - AND their friend would get a special first-time discount too.

I would have a "Hair Cut Sale" - deeply discounted prices for hair cuts during the slow times of the week, month or year.

Maybe have "Buy 2, Get 1 Free" offers, to encourage women to come in groups for a cut. Maybe this would encourage the customers to pull in fellow workers or friends who aren't already a customer. Nice way to get new leads.

Create web software that they can use to experiment with different hair styles and hair colors using their own picture. Maybe have a "Celebrity Styles" section where they can see on the computer, what they would look like with a celebrity's hair style.

I would sign up for top-notch hair products as an affiliate, and send relevant affiliate links in my emails embedded in short stories or articles I write, and these links would bring me some additional revenue in affiliate commissions.

Well, you get the idea.

The brainstorming above took me about 5 minutes. How much more could you come up with if this was really your own hair salon, and you put some serious effort into thinking of ways to add value to your service using your web site?

If you sold electronic goods, your web site should have all owner's manuals, technical guides, troubleshooting tips, online chat for technical support, product specifications, large (really large) high resolution pictures, online-only discounts, FAQ's, Knowledge Base, and user forums where users can answer other users' questions too.

Another plus to getting going with blogging, is that you will get a feel for being a "web site owner". You will notice how it is easy to get your first few visitors (some of your friends, few of your relatives, and mom, of course), and also how difficult it is to get past those few and get new visitors to come visit your web site.

You should also sign up for Google Adsense (see chapter "How To Earn A Nice Little Paycheck From Google"), and you will soon start to realize that getting your visitors to click on your ads, is even more difficult than getting them over to your site in the first place.

So, as you dive head-long into web site building and working on your new "blog", you will learn quickly about what works and what doesn't work, and what kind of revenue model you want to pursue.

So head over to Blogger.com or Wordpress.com and setup your free account today. But wait, just finish the rest of this book first – there are some tips you just can't afford to miss – things you are better off getting right the first time around.

11. How To Get Paid Online

You have gone grocery shopping.

Your shopping cart is full of groceries and household items that you want to purchase.

You go to the checkout counter.

The cashier adds up all your items and the total amount comes to $85.

You pull out your credit card to pay the amount.

The cashier apologizes and tells you with a straight face that they accept only cashier's checks and money orders – and then tells you to go to the post office round the corner, get a cashier's check or money order for $85, come back to the store, and then pay for your groceries.

Sorry, he won't even take personal checks.

How would you feel?

Never make your customer feel the same way. If you make it inconvenient and a hassle for your customers to pay you, you can kiss the sale goodbye.

You must absolutely provide your customers the ability to pay you at web site using their credit or debit card – or even an electronic check.

Make it easy for your visitor to get information about your products, contact you easily if they have pre- or post- sales questions, a convenient and secure way to pay instantly, and a no-hassle 100% refund guarantee.

If they have a positive experience at your web site, your visitors are then more likely to recommend you to others even if they don't buy from you right away. And most of them are likely to bookmark your web site and return again soon to eventually purchase your product.

How soon they return, can be influenced by your follow-up emails.

Accepting Credit Cards On Your Site

There are two ways you can go about accepting credit card payments on your web site.

Using a third party: The best (and cheapest) option for those just starting out or for those with lower level sales (<$1000 per month).

Using your own merchant account: More expensive to get started, but definitely recommended for long term (and a must once your business takes off).

Using a Third-Party

These third-parties are also commonly known as aggregators. Some of the more popular ones are Paypal, 2Checkout.com, ClickBank .

These are all online services, which don't require you to have your own merchant account. All you will need to do is to sign up for an account online with these providers - almost like signing up for a free email account at hotmail or yahoo. Some may also require a minimal one-time fee to join (Paypal is free).

Advantages of using a 3rd-party processor:

1. Free or almost free:

Paypal.com	Free
ClickBank.com	$49.95 (one time)
2Checkout.com	$49.00 (one time)
Google Checkout	Free

2. **Quick start**: You can almost always start selling within a few hours of signing up for an account (sometimes it may take up to 48 hours before your account is activated; or you may need to be specially enabled to sell high ticket items, as with ClickBank).

3. **No recurring, monthly fees**: Your fees are only based on your sales. So if you sell nothing, you pay them nothing.

4. **No minimum commissions or penalties**: Commissions are charged only on sales that you make. There are no penalties for low sales either. So, like I mentioned above, if you don't make even one single sale in a month, then you incur no additional fees at the end of the month (of course, you will still have to pay their one-time sign up fee).

5. **Internationally available**: Paypal (at last count) was available in some 40+ countries, and ClickBank and 2Checkout accept merchants from almost anywhere in the whole world. If you are in a country other than US or Canada, the only disadvantage is that you will be sent a check by regular mail - which could take a while depending on which part of the world you live in. And the other thing to remember is that payment is still in US dollars, which I am sure most banks in most parts of the world welcome, and would gladly convert into local currency for you.

Processing payments through a third-party is probably the best option if you are just starting out and want to feel the waters before you dive-in, or if you have average sales and are still growing.

Like all things in life, there is always a price to pay for the choices we make - even when the lunch is free :-)

Disadvantages of Using a 3rd-Party Processor

1. **Higher commissions**:

More expenses mean fewer dollars in your pocket.

For instance, ClickBank charges a whopping fee of 7.5% of the total sale price *PLUS* a transaction fee of $1.00. So, if you sold an ebook for $100, ClickBank will keep $8.50, leaving you with $91.50 in profits. The $8.50 you lost in commissions may not seem like much if you are just starting out. However, multiply that by hundreds of sales, and you will see what I meant when I labeled it as the No. 1 disadvantage.

2. **Not very customer friendly**:

The confirmation email is usually sent from the aggregator's web site. Which means, in all probability, if your customer has a problem, the first email that they respond to is the aggregator's email. Also, the customer's interaction is with a representative of the third-party processor, and their experience may or may not be as pleasant or smooth as you would like it to be.

And you certainly have NO control over complaints or even minor dissatisfactions, which could be easily solved if the customer had approached you first.

Also, offering timely support and service could be another issue, if there is a time delay in the payment processor relaying the customer's request to you.

3. **Not brand friendly**:

You won't look very professional if the transaction receipt email is from a third-party web site, and not from your own email address having your own branding, wording and customer service and other self-help information.

4. **Not merchant friendly**:

ClickBank, for instance, has this rather ridiculous option (from a merchant's perspective) where if a buyer wants a refund for whatever reason, all she has to do to is simply forward their transaction confirmation email back to ClickBank - and they are refunded instantly - NO QUESTIONS ASKED.

The entire transaction happens without involving the seller in any way, and the buyer is not even required to provide *any* explanation as to why they are opting for a refund.

If they have an issue that they require help with (for instance, if their browser had crashed and they were unable to download your digital product, or they have a after-sales question about the product), the seller is not even given a chance to offer support or rectify the problem, if any.

The seller is instead just notified by email *after* a refund has occurred, and sometimes the buyer's original email requesting a refund is not even forwarded to the buyer until much later - or sometimes not at all!

On the surface, this may look like these services are offering great buyer-protection, but what they are actually doing is encouraging hijackers and pirates to rip off honest and sincere merchants, by allowing scumbags to purchase a product, and almost immediately, within minutes, request for a refund, without giving the seller a chance to resolve any issues that they may have.

There have been cases when I have checked my email to find both the sale notification and the refund notification (of a refund that has already been processed and the money debited from my account) emails together in my inbox, one below the other, barely minutes apart from each other.

5. **Not very customizable or re-brandable**:

You've got to live with the features offered by these services. Some of them offer limited additional technology to enhance the sales process, but these extras are not nearly as useful you or your customer would like it to be.

Using Your Own Merchant Account

Getting your own merchant account is definitely a more elaborate process than signing up with a third-party processor. It may involve a bank or financial institution, and expect some paperwork, policies and guidelines to be met with and followed, and approvals required from the bank folks. However, if you are not a beginner, and already have a decent flow of sales, then this may be the perfect upgrade for your business - in order to look more professional, have better control over customer service and support, and better control over your refunds.

Advantages of Having Your Own Merchant Account:

1. **Lower commissions**: You can get merchant account providers (providers) who charge as little 2.10% per transaction (compared to ClickBank's 7.5%) and a few cents per transaction - about $0.25 (25 cents, compared to ClickBank's $1).

In business, every dollar counts. When you start selling more, a 5% savings in costs like commission fees can make a tremendous difference to your bottom-line.

2. **Very customer friendly**: You own the account. You charge your customer. You handle sales and support.

You are the one dealing with your customer, every step of the way. This means, you maintain your brand identity, and can put your best foot forward.

3. **Very merchant friendly**: Since you also handle refunds, you can pretty much put an end to all those buy-download-and-get-a-refund-in-3-minutes kind of customers. I personally saw a nearly 95% decline in fraud ever since I switched to my own merchant account after using both ClickBank and 2Checkout.com.

Of course, having your own merchant does not take away fraudulent purchases made using stolen credit cards. But that's a risk you will be taking in any business - and you are better off if you have a digital product, because you didn't really lose any money on shipping or handling.

4. **Highly configurable & customizable**: Since you own the process, you can control the user experience to a major extent. For instance, you can pick the e-Commerce software of your choice. You could go for free shopping carts like OSCommerce, or go for a full-featured online service like 1SiteAutomation.com - which comes with a suite of integrated services like autoresponders, shopping cart, bulk-mailing, affiliate program, campaign tracking, etc.

Going for a full-service system will not only save you a lot of headache and effort and maintenance costs in trying to figure out everything and install everything from scratch on your site, but will also free you up from all those non-value adding chores, giving you more time to focus on the real task at hand, which is marketing your existing products or services and creating new ones.

Disadvantages of Having Your Own Merchant Account

1. **Comes at a cost:** You may have to pay one-time set up charges (though providers may waive them sometimes), and monthly recurring costs could be $15 to $30 even if you don't make one single sale the entire month.

2. **Involves paper work:** Set up may take a few days and also require you to sign some agreements and require approvals from the financial institution before you can make that first sale.

3. **Not everyone may be eligible or get the same pricing:** If you are an individual just starting out, you may have to show more documentation. Even after all the paper work, your application could still be rejected if you have very bad credit or have claimed bankruptcy in the recent past.

If you live outside the United States or Canada, it may be a lot more difficult to get a merchant account from a US bank or processor. Even if you do get approved, you may end up paying higher set up fees and recurring charges. Best option is to contact your local banks and credit card processors.

4. **Miscellaneous Charges Can Add Up Real Quick**: There will be costs involved in providing customer support for transactions and refunds and the like. You will also need your own e-Commerce set up to handle all the transactions, customer calls, bank enquiries, etc.

So What Should You Choose?

The bottom-line: If you are testing the waters, or are just starting out, you may not want to be bogged down by infrastructure costs and effort, and may be better off outsourcing your credit card processing to third-party processors like Paypal or ClickBank.

I highly recommend going with ClickBank rather than Paypal, because ClickBank can accept regular credit card payments as well as Paypal payments (from Paypal members). Plus ClickBank comes with a readily available army of web site owners who will willingly promote your product for a share of the.

Don't worry about paying extra in commissions and the higher per-sale fee to ClickBank. When you are starting out, you will have minimal sales, and having this army of ClickBank affiliates on your side can only help get the word out about your product. And the additional fees they charge will more than make up in terms of the reduced effort in dealing with refunds and chargebacks and paying your affiliates and keeping track of all of those payments and accounting.

However, if you already have a web site and have a decent stream of sales, and are ready to take your business to the next level in terms of appearing more professional and global, and want more control over your business, then the advantages of having your own merchant account cannot be overstated.

Accepting Payments using ClickBank

ClickBank is an extremely popular, fast growing merchant-account service provider – who is popular for a lot of reasons.

They were among the first to introduce pay-as-you-go accounts for accepting credit card payments online. They have a small, one-time sign up fee of $49. After that, it is pay as you go – which means, if you don't sell anything, you don't pay any fees. When you do sell, they take a percentage (7.5% actually) of that sale.

7.5% may seem like a lot at first – but remember you are not paying any fixed monthly fees, no extras like gateway fees, batch processing fees, etc. Just $1 + 7.5% of the sale. So, if you sold an e-book for $10, ClickBank would take $1 + $0.75 = $1.75 as their commissions, and pay you $8.25.

Hey, that's not too bad considering you have almost no investment, no maintenance fees, and you are paying only *after* you have made the sale. No sale, no fees - remember?

The biggest advantage (and arguably, also their biggest disadvantage) of using ClickBank is their hugely popular affiliate program. They have made it so outrageously easy for anyone to promote any merchant's products that people could be promoting your products on their web site and you may not even be aware of it.

Every merchant who sells through ClickBank gets their product automatically added to the affiliate program – which means any and all of ClickBank's existing and future affiliates will be able to sell your product. The good thing about making the affiliate program so easy is that you, as a merchant, get a readily available army of 100,000+ affiliates who will compete with each other to promote your product on their web site and newsletter, in return for a portion of your profits, of course.

On the other hand, because ClickBank and its affiliate program is so powerful, if you are selling products or services targeted at e-Businesses and web site owners, like my own WebmasterInABox.net for example, then you could be pretty much certain that most of your target audience will be a ClickBank affiliate themselves, and would probably use their own affiliate link for their own purchase, which means, they are forcefully taking a big chunk out of your profits to keep for themselves as a self-earned discount.

The bottom-line is that it is possible that many of these affiliates may not have purchased your products if you had not been selling through ClickBank. So, it is better to have some profits than no profits.

A PHP script - the "ClickBank Download Protector" (a $34.95 value) from the WebmasterInABox.net Toolkit - is included for free in the NBLEB Toolkit. It will help you protect your digital products that you sell through ClickBank. It includes detailed installation instructions, and comes with free technical support.

Working with ClickBank

Visit ClickBank's web site at www.ClickBank.com

To sell using ClickBank (CB), you need to first sign up for a free account with them, by going to Clickbank.com/signup. The CB username you chose during signup (referred to as "nickname" by CB) can be used for both for selling digital products as well as for referring visitors to other web sites and earning commissions on referred sales (referred to as affiliate sales).

If you are just going to be using CB as an affiliate, then there are no fees. However, if you are going to sell products using CB, then you have to pay a one-time fee of $49.95. Other than this, there are no monthly fees, and you will then just be paying a small portion of your sales as the sales fees, only when you make a sale.

Also, if your sale was referred by one of your affiliates, then CB automatically pays the affiliate the due commissions as specified by you.

So **sale price** minus **CB fees** minus **affiliate commissions** is credited to your account, and you can specify in your account a minimum threshold dollar amount upon the reaching of which CB will send you a physical check in the mail.

Accepting Payments using Paypal

Paypal (www.Paypal.com) was one of the first services to allow people to pay anyone else with an email address, and currently you can send money to anyone living in about 190 countries and regions where Paypal is accepted.

Just enter the recipient's email address and the amount you wish to send and send a payment from a linked bank account or credit card. One of the biggest advantages of Paypal is that it has a huge user base (about 78 million users at last count), is available in 56 countries, and is owned by eBay, which by itself is a giant in ecommerce.

Another big plus is that it is free, and there are no upfront costs to set up a seller's account. You will however be paying a small portion of any sales you make, only when the actual sale is made. Otherwise, there are no upfront, monthly or recurring fees.

The advantage with offering Paypal as a payment option on your site, is that those who are already a Paypal member will be able to complete the purchase real swiftly, as they just need to enter their Paypal account username and password, and click on a confirmation button to complete the purchase. They don't need to enter any long payment forms or enter any credit card information.

Paypal can be a great choice of payment to offer on your web site along with your other regular forms of payments. For those of your visitors who are already Paypal members, check-out and paying you will be a breeze. So, if you are not currently accepting payments on your web site, then Paypal will be a great first choice, especially if you want to start with zero upfront cost.

And as you grow bigger, you can always retain Paypal as one of the payment options among others.

Paypal IPN (Instant Payment Notification)

Paypal offers a secure payment notification system which can be used to confirm for sure that a payment has actually been made to your account, before releasing the purchased digital product online, or to automate various aspects of the purchase.

Check out the detailed article I've written about this at `Webmasterinabox.net/paypal_ipn.html`

What I Use

I use both ClickBank and Paypal, but for my main web sites where I need more control over the payments, I use a merchant account and the integrated shopping cart suite 1SiteAutomation.com.

When I first started out doing business online, I was living in India (now I live in Westchester County, NY), and the first processor (credit card processor) I used was CCNow.com. They were free to join at that time – but had extremely high commissions (9% of the sale!), but they were the only ones who allowed International merchants to participate.

They are no longer free - they apparently charge a $9.95 sign up fee, $0.50 per sale, and 4.99% of the gross in commissions. What seems discouraging even now is that if you sell less than $100 per month, you will have to pay them a monthly fee of $9.95. Check their site for details.

I haven't used them since the days of their 9% commissions, so I am not in a position to recommend them at this time.

I have extensively used ClickBank and 2Checkout, but they always had their own limitations and I eventually out-grew them. Finally, in 2002, I switched to my own merchant account.

If you are just starting out, don't worry about the hassles of a merchant account; look no further than ClickBank.com – because they have no monthly fees, a readily available army of affiliates to promote your product, their per-transaction fees and commissions are not too bad either, and they even allow customers with a Paypal account to pay for your product using their Paypal funds.

See TrueMerchantAccount.com for a detailed report on payment processors.

12. Internet Marketing

Ok, you have a web site, *and* a product. Now what?

How are you going promote it? How would any one know who you are, where you are, or why they should really care about your product?

You've got to get the word out. Now that you have a working web site and a product, your goals are clear-cut:

- Get new leads: Increase traffic from your target market to your web site
- Improve conversion from visitor to customer
- Offer up-sells and cross-promotions to increase value of each sale
- Offer backend products to increase sales
- Offer a way for them to recommend you – preferably through your affiliate program which will also give them an incentive to recommend you to others.
- Ask for feedback, keep your eyes and ears open for new opportunities
- Continue to improve your current product based on feedback.

- Continue to develop new products for target market – once again based on feedback - to offer as add-ons, incentives or just plain backend products.

There's more to this than listed above, but you get the big picture.

The term "Internet marketing" is probably the most over-rated, over-used, nauseatingly abused, two words online. You can find any number of courses and web sites online that will "bring millions of visitors overnight" or sell "millions of email addresses for a few dollars", "send your sales through the roof" or "fill your pockets with wads of cash" or help you "laugh all the way to the bank".

Trust me - none of those work. But rather than criticize what *they* are doing, let us focus on what *you* need to do, to start making money off of *your* web site.

13. List Building

When was the last time, you went to a web site looking for a particular product or service, clicked the "Buy Now" button, opened your wallet and shelled out the money - all during your first visit?

Probably never.

Few people will plunk down their credit card online the first time they visit a web site. Whether they buy from you at all, depends on how urgent their need is, how well your product matches the solution they are looking for, how professional and convincing and "real" your copy and your language is, and/or how trustworthy you seem.

But as a general rule of thumb, people don't purchase a product until they have been exposed to your site, newsletter, or advertisement, about 7 times.

If you want to be even remotely successful online, you will need to build what is called a "mailing list" – no, not the postal office kind, but the "email" kind.

This is a list of people who have "opted" to receive email communications from you, on a topic of their interest. This list could just have people wanting to be notified when you update content on your site, or those who want to receive your weekly newsletter where you share tips and tricks relevant to your industry, relevant to their need *at that time*. Or this could simply be a list of your current customers, potential customers (leads) or just people who have an interest in anything you may want to say.

You need to keep in touch with your site visitors, mailing list subscribers and customers, so that you can remind them about your web site's existence, make them come back often, build a relationship, and eventually sell them more of your products.

Make sure these folks have voluntarily asked to receive emails from you. Send unsolicited email, and you will have your subscribers screaming S-P-A-M – the ugly term given for such unsolicited emails – and your business may get into trouble for this.

The government has even passed a law that can punish offenders with thousands of (US) dollars in fines.

Also, make sure you have something interesting or relevant to say. Send them junk even 1 out of 10 times, and you'll see a flurry of people un-subscribing (leaving your list) – and even expect that occasional hate email too.

Your Subscriber – Your Golden Goose

It is difficult selling to a stranger, but much simpler selling to a friend.

Don't mean to say start hitting up all of your friends with sales calls. Remember, the fastest way to lose friends is to pitch them Amway or Quixtar.

Let's say you have a web site getting 50,000 visitors a month. And you have a newsletter with 500 subscribers.

It's easier to earn a dollar in sales from your 500 subscribers, than it is with your 50,000 visitors.

Don't get caught up in the numbers game. Number of visitors, number of hits to your web site, number of page views – all these numbers don't mean squat if you don't have any sales.

Most companies from the dot-bomb era failed precisely because of this. They purchased eyeballs and visitors and hits and page views in the millions – with extensive advertising, expensive advertising (it costs up to a million dollars for 10 seconds of ad time during the Superbowl, America's most watched television event).

But they did not have a revenue model in place. They had all those millions of visitors coming in, but they did not have a way to "monetize" all that traffic – all they cared for were the numbers – the number of registered users - which would eventually help a handful of those e-Businesses to sell out to the big guys for millions of dollars.

The rest just withered and died.

No matter how expensive and professional looking your web site is, if you are not developing a relationship with your site visitors, then you have almost very little chance of succeeding in ebusiness.

You can read a hundred books on marketing, go attend any number of expensive seminars and courses, and join any number of private clubs that teach how to make more money. In the end, it pretty much comes down to one thing: Your mailing list.

So, take a deep breath, close your eyes, and repeat after me three times, slowly exhaling and inhaling each time...

"The money is in the list..."

"The money is in the list..."

"The money is in the list..."

If you *really* got this one, you could pretty much stop reading this book right now. But there are other little things that you will need to make the list building work, so I recommend you finish reading the rest of this book.

Give Me One Reason Why...

Email addresses have become so much more personal today, than they were a few years ago. Today, asking your site's visitor for their email address is like asking a girl who you just ran into at a bar, for her home phone number.

There's very little chance that you'll get it, unless you give her a very strong reason.

What is her motivation? Why should she give you her private contact information? Give me one reason why.

Offer an incentive. More importantly, offer a "relevant" incentive.

Imagine striking up a conversation with this girl at the bar, and telling her that your mother's uncle served in Vietnam. Why would she care? Instead if you had said you were in the army yourself, or that you were a cop, or a firefighter, or had an interesting story or two to tell about your own life experiences, then there's a much better chance of that conversation going somewhere. Make it relevant. Your visitor has come to your site for only one reason – hoping you have something that will help solve their problem.

You could throw in a freebie that is related to your product, and use this freebie as an incentive for them to sign up for your newsletter. And promise them more valuable freebies – relevant information, related information, exclusive, subscribers-only discounts for your products, alerts notifying them of the latest happenings in your industry - anything that is related to what they are looking for.

For instance, my site WebmasterInABox.net is about computer programs – also known as scripts. People come to my site in search of scripts that will help them solve a programming need without having to hire an expensive programmer. What better incentive for them than a few free scripts that they can't find elsewhere?

I use free scripts as a bonus to persuade them to subscribe to my newsletter. And a few times a month, I send them not just free scripts I developed myself, but also information other high quality free products and services that I use, or have used myself.

Continuing to deliver quality information over a period of time, will help you establish a relationship with your subscribers. If your information helps them solve a problem or learn something new, then they will begin to view you as an expert in your industry – and when they are ready to buy products or services related to what you are selling, guess who is the first person they think of? You, of course!

Over the years, I have received many emails from subscribers who received my newsletters for many months, and then eventually purchased my products, and sent me emails "thanking" me for the helpful information that had sent them, and mentioning how I had finally been able to persuade them to purchase my scripts.

These people came to my site as complete strangers. They came to my site from all parts of the world, and at the time of writing this book, I don't even have a picture of myself on my site.

In spite of knowing nothing about me, these strangers who had signed up voluntarily to receive my newsletter mostly because I offered them free scripts, had eventually warmed up to me, trusted me, had a relationship with me, and were comfortable enough to purchase something from me online.

All because I had put in time, effort and knowledge in my newsletters – to send them valuable information that they could use.

Bottom-line: Your subscribers hold the key to your fortune. Build your list and keep them happy - they will lead you to riches.

Don't Abuse the Goose

You have probably heard about the goose that laid golden eggs. Remember what happened? The man got greedy and killed the goose hoping to get all the eggs at one go.

You can expect the same fat if you abuse your subscribers by sending them too much email too soon – you will be left holding an empty list (dead goose). Sending them junk-pretending-to-be-content is sure to start a snowballing flurry of visitors canceling their subscription to your newsletter (a.k.a "unsubscribing"). They will not just unsubscribe – some may even go the extent of bashing you publicly in their own newsletters, blogs (web logs) or other online forums.

You would have lost not just a subscriber, but many future dollars in potential sales – not to mention, your reputation – which is harder to earn than money itself.

Everything lies in balancing the *Content-to-Sales Pitch* ratio. Email not too often, not too far apart. Not too little content, not too many ads. Not overtly hip, not too serious. Not too many freebies, not too much fluff.

You can get a better idea about this balance, simply by subscribing to a few *really good lists* yourself. Observe their timing, the amount of personalization (does the email start by addressing you by your name), the content-to-pitch ratio (amount of content compared to the number of sales pitches in each edition), ease of subscribing and unsubscribing, the content of the subject line, the existence and display of a privacy policy and so on.

Spam: Weapon of Mass Destruction

When was the last time you purchased something from a telemarketer who intruded on your privacy by calling you in when you were having dinner with your family, pronounced your name wrong, didn't care to ask if this were a good time to call you, asked you the fakest "how are you doing today", and dived right into a sales pitch for some stupid credit card or phone offer without the slightest regard for your time or your interest?

That's how people will feel if you send them your newsletter or sales pitch without their permission.

Seth Godin, the author of the best seller, "Permission Marketing" (who also happens to be the one who coined that word) puts it beautifully, when he says "Permission marketing turns strangers into friends and friends into loyal customers".

Spam is nothing but `Unsolicited Commercial Email` (UCE). Anytime you send someone a commercial email without their *permission*, it is considered as "spamming them". In fact, the email doesn't even have to be commercial in nature – you can spam your friends simply by sending them funny (to you) but unwanted (to them) jokes, or large images that clog up their email addresses.

But this acceptable form of spamming friends and family is what gave birth to the concept of "Viral Marketing" – better understood as "word of mouth marketing" - an extremely powerful and persuasive technique used by savvy marketing professionals where they rely on people who buy the product or service to tell friends and family.

The idea is to get them so excited about the product or service, that they not only just tell friends and family, but in fact even go to the extent of persuading the people to know to do just the same.

Why Publish a Newsletter (a.k.a. E-zine)?

Newsletters are a very powerful tool when it comes to establishing trust, keeping in touch, keeping your brand at the forefront of your potential customers' mind so that they think you first (or among the first few) when they want (or need) whatever it is that you are selling.

Newsletters can be used to publish content relevant to your industry, focused on the product you are selling, and help build traffic and as a consequence, generate qualified leads.

You can archive your newsletters online, which can improve your site's ranking in search results on various search engines due to many factors – due to fresh new content being published regularly, due to keyword-rich copy which may end up as a match during a search for a non-optimized keyword that appears naturally in your content, and due to other sites viewing you as an authority site and linking to you with one-way links, and due to other sites and directories that have a similar theme as yours linking to your site as a way of providing their visitors with additional resources on the subject.

You can even make money by allowing others to syndicate your content (meaning, publish your content on their web site, or by re-publishing it as a part of their newsletter), and can even make a career out of it, much like syndicated newspaper and magazine columnists.

Not to forget that newsletters can bring in advertisement and affiliate revenue – or you can sell more of your own products as you chip away at the apprehension of your potential customer with each edition, proving with each issue why your product is the best answer to their problem.

What to Publish?

Regardless of what you publish, remember that the whole idea of a newsletter is to get leads, convert those leads into sales, and to keep bringing your customers back to buy more.

Original Content

If you have your own product, you are probably an expert in your field. So your newsletter content could (and should) revolve around your product.

Offer tips, tricks, "insider info", freebies, expert insight, opinions, guidance, support, help (answering your readers' questions) and practical how-to's - literally anything and everything to do with your product's subject area.

Remember, if you are selling *Product A*, then you should publish a newsletter focused on *Product A*, and sign up people who are interesting in knowing more about *Product A*, and develop content for the kind of people who would need *Product A*.

So, if you're selling bathroom furnishings, then you could write about home maintenance, bathroom furnishing and decoration, bathroom repair and maintenance and related tools and equipment.

Guest Articles

If you are short on content or time, you can always publish articles from other authors. There are any number of web site owners who are looking to syndicate their content – mostly for free – in order to get exposure to their product and brand.

Most will gladly allow you to publish their article or write-up for free, as long as you honor their re-printing guidelines, which would usually just require you to give them credit for their article by retaining their signature (a small blurb of text at the end of the article promoting their product or web site, also called as the 'tag-line').

But be warned, publishing too many guest articles will make you look like you don't know enough, or like you don't care enough to spend time creating your own content.

Professional direct marketers rarely use guest articles. Instead, you could research the topic you are writing about on Google.com, and you could use various quotes and facts from different articles, web sites and books, as long as you credit them appropriately.

This way, you would have managed to use third-party content, without making you look like a copy-paste writer, while at the same time, including enough all-round research information that shows you know what you are talking about.

To get a better idea, read articles on News.com, or blogs of famous authors like Seth Godin.

Articles with Affiliate Links

You can also publish articles that have been specifically written to promote a product – and are tied into an affiliate program such that the article contains your give you an added incentive help you make money – like marketer Jim Edwards' newsletters that lets you replace the sales page link (of the product being promoted) with your own affiliate link (you will have to sign up to be Jim's affiliate first, of course).

Opt-In vs. Opt-Out

Opt-in when people specifically ask to receive your newsletter – like signing up through a form on your web site. In this case, you only send them the newsletter that they "voluntarily" signed up for, and not any other content, even though you may have multiple other newsletters that you publish.

Opt-out is when you sign up someone by default – that is, *force* them into receiving your newsletter - when they are signing up for a diffeent service. This can happen in a number of ways – one famous example is many years ago, when you signed up for a Hotmail.com account many years ago, you were automatically subscribed to a number of MSN newsletters.

During that time, I used to run an Internet café, and I remember helping some customers sign up for a hotmail account, and then after a few months, they would ask me for help in deleting hundreds of emails from all the "Opt-out" spam that MSN was sending them, and none of them ever knew what those emails were, or why they were getting them in the first place.

I even ran a test where I signed up for a Hotmail email account with a ridiculous user name (with all kinds of text and numbers in it), and used all the default options given to me when signing up (like leaving alone all the pre-checked check boxes during the signup process) – and when I logged back in many months later, I found hundreds of emails in my inbox.

All of this without ever sending or receiving a single email from that account, not giving out the email address to anyone, and not doing anything but just using the default sign up options).

Hotmail eventually changed that policy, and I haven't checked in the last, say, um, 8 years to see if they reverted back to their spammy policy or not (I'm guessing *not*, given the hyper-spam-sensitive society we live in these days).

Yahoo has also been under fire previously for auto-signing up people for services and content, just because they were signing up for something else.

Yahoo and MSN can probably get away with it – not you. So don't ever force or trick your users into signing up for something they never asked for. If they signed up for your newsletter on pregnancy, doesn't mean you can automatically start sending them your newsletter on cosmetic procedures.

Publishing Tips

Personalized Emails

People like a personal touch. Blockbuster, the movie rental chain, promises you a free rental, if the counter clerk doesn't call you by first name when you check out.

Emails that have the reader's first name in the subject and message greeting, tend to get opened a lot more than non-personalized, generic, bulk-mail type of emails.

You don't have to manually send each of your subscribers an individual email to accomplish this – there is software available that will insert the subscriber's first name at the time of sending out the email (a.k.a mail-merge) and allow you to send thousands of personalized emails, just as if you were emailing each of them personally.

Subject Line

The subject line is like a newspaper headline, like an advertisement's headline - very crucial for getting your email opened.

You may even want to attach a short acronym for your newsletter (for ex., I use the tag {SNS} for my newsletter "Scripts-n-Software") followed by the actual subject, which servers two purposes – one it lets your reader create a filter that puts all emails with the text {SNS} into a special folder, to archive it for later or just to make sure it doesn't get mixed up with the rest.

It also gets your visitor used to seeing that tag in the subject line over a period of time, and if you serve quality content regularly, they may even look forward to your email and over a period of time, associate the niche that you are in, with your name.

Newsletter Copy Width

Try to keep this within 60-65 characters per line, so that your subscriber doesn't see ugly line breaks when they read your newsletter in their email client (Eudora, Outlook or Gmail).

Publishing (Somewhat) Frequently

It is important that you send out your newsletters with some level of frequency. Those who like receiving your content, will look forward to it, and sending them in a timely fashion will get a higher response from your offer (if you are making one in your newsletter, along with your content – and I recommend that along with good content, every email you send out should have some kind of an offer – be it free, or for fee).

Also, if you allow too much time between newsletters, it is possible that your subscribers may forget about their subscription to your newsletter, and may mistakenly flag it as spam. Trust me, it has happened to me and the consequences were nasty, ugly and terribly inconvenient.

Links and Email Addresses

Prepend all email addresses in your newsletter body with the text mailto: (ex., mailto:Ravi@NBLEB.com).

Prepend all domain names with http:// (ex., http://www.NBLEB.com).

Doing this will make sure all email addresses and links are "clickable" – meaning, the mouse pointer turns into a "hand" when moved over the email id or link, which makes it easy for your reader to simply click on, say if they wanted to send you an email or visit that link.

This tip is not applicable to most email clients (especially web-based ones like Gmail and Yahoo), but is still worth following for the few remaining clients that don't automatically make the email addresses and links "clickable".

Also, enclose long links within the "<" and ">" text so that the link doesn't wrap around and break into two different links (which might corrupt the original link, making it unusable or invalid). Ex: http://NBLEB.com/this-is-a-very-long-link.php?q=there-is-a-lot-more-text-coming

You may encounter such links when deep linking into a web site, or say, when using affiliate links.

Standard Headers and Footers

A standard *header* would be something where you inform the reader something about the newsletter and why they are receiving it. For example:

"Hello Ravi,

You are receiving this newsletter because you voluntarily subscribed by visiting our web site at http://www.NBLEB.com. If you wish to change your subscription options or wish to unsubscribe, please see the links at the end of this newsletter."

Similarly, a *footer* would look like this:

"This email is never sent unsolicited. To change your subscription options or unsubscribe, click on the link below:

http://www.NBLEB.com/leave.php?e=a@b.com"

(Of course, a good autoresponder program would encrypt the email address at the end of the above link, and also send a confirmation message to the subscriber asking for confirmation whether they really want to leave the list.)

You should also provide them with a mailing address, in case your links don't work, or if they want to unsubscribe from all of your lists, rather than just the one they are reading (assuming you publish multiple newsletters). That could read something like:

"To be removed from all our lists, you can also write to:
REMOVE ALL
PO Box 12345, Some city, State 09876"

Un-Subscription Links

See the "Standard header and footer" section above.

Testing Delivery and Format

You may have noticed many emails that come with an empty subject, or incorrectly merged text where your name or salutation should've been, badly formatted text or HTML, missing images, invalid links (pointing to a local `c:\` drive instead of to a web site), and so on.

These are almost always the result of not testing the basic newsletter by sending it to one-self before sending it out to others.

Create a small 'test' group on the same service as your actual ezine .

For example, if you are using yahoogroups.com to send your ezine/newsletter, then create another group called 'test-ezine' (or whatever name you get) and add about 5-10 different email addresses of your own, as subscribers.

Let this "test group" have a good variety; add ids @hotmail.com, @yahoo.com, @gmail.com, @NBLEB.com etc - to the test group.

When the newsletter is ready to be published, send it to this test group first, and check to see how it is delivered. If yours is a HTML newsletter, you may be surprised to learn that sometimes the same ezine can look pretty different in different email clients, like Gmail, Yahoo, Outlook and Eudora - and we're not even talking about different browsers here when it comes to web mail.

You will also be surprised to learn that, after you've checked out your *final* version using the above test group, you will still get some more ideas for tweaking your ezine just that little bit more.

If you change anything whatsoever after you ran your first test, you have to test again. Yup, every time you make the smallest change to the content, you need to repeat the test mailing - you have no idea how a seemingly trivial change can screw things up.

After your final mailing to your test group, after you've made sure everything's just perfect, *without* touching the source of your newsletter, just paste it into your actual ezine compose box, and hit send.

Promoting Your Newsletter

Creating a powerful, valuable newsletter is just one half of the equation. The next thing you need to do is to get people - lots of people - to sign up for it.

Creating Remarkable Content

Let's start with the hardest way – which is also the most powerful way: creating remarkable content that people will want to share with others and do the promoting for you, for free.

When you have great content, people will fall over each other. This applies to both web sites and newsletters and just about any content you develop (even books you write).

Compare this to Apple's iPod. You don't need to convince people to buy an iPod. If they have a need for a portable music player, they probably already have one. You don't need heavy marketing, no free bonuses or bribes required, no buy-1-get-1 offers necessary. People all over the world have made iPods a huge hit, in spite of the heavy price tag compared to so many other digital content players.

To quote the famously incorrect usage of a famous saying, "build a better mouse trap, and the world will beat a path to your door".

Offering a Powerful, Free Bonus

The most popular way, and also the (relatively) easiest way to get more people to sign up, is to offer them a bribe. Not just any bribe, but something closely related to the theme of your product, service or web site – something that your target audience – who are also your potential customers – will be interested in.

When I got started with my site WebmasterInABox.net, for a long time, I was just offering some ridiculous freebies – it was probably a free ebook, or some third-party software that was promoting somebody else's web site!

It was after reading Stephen Pierce's "The Whole Truth" ebook that I realized, that if I were to create this free bonus myself, it would be infinitely more powerful, as it would be more relevant to my potential buyers than offering some one else's software or ebook, it could also do my marketing for me long after they've downloaded the free bonus (in the form of a back-link from a ebook that I wrote, or from footer links from the free scripts I developed), plus it would help get me plenty of back-links from other web sites that would refer their visitors and subscribers to "Go download this Free Affiliate Link Cloaker Script" from my site, which would in turn raise my PageRank™, which would mean higher positioning in search engine results.

So, try to spend some time, effort and even some money in creating a free bonus as an incentive for your subscribers, because if your free bonus is very similar or an add-on or an extension of your main product that you are actually selling, it could provide a great incentive for them to purchase your main product, as your free bonus would only complement your main product or service.

Free bonuses are commonly used not just for generating new subscribers for your newsletter, but for generating leads (potential buyers) for just about any product or service, online or offline.

Using Pop-Ups

Everybody hates pop-ups. Well, almost everyone. But guess what, nothing converts like pop-ups, because pop-ups are in-your-face, and it's hard to miss them!

So, use pop-ups carefully, as sites like Google will disallow your site from displaying Adsense ads if your site throws pop-ups in your visitors' face. You could use time-delayed DHTML pop-ups (that are a lot more subtle than new-window pop-ups) and see if your visitors are more responsive to that.

The bottom-line however is that the more web-savvy your target audience is, the more they will hate your pop-ups and may even leave your site altogether to never come back. The less web-savvy your visitors are (mom-and-pop niche sites built for the average person), the more they tend to tolerate pop-ups. But the number of *un-savvy* people is dwindling fast, so all you can do is to experiment and track the results.

Using Co-Registration

Co-registration is a strategy where you trade newsletter sign-up forms or just web site links to your newsletter's sign up page, with other newsletter publishers or web site owners. The location of the exchanged form or link would be the "thank you" page of the site owner's main subscription page.

For instance, once a visitor signs up for your newsletter, you would normally show them a "thank you for subscribing, your newsletter is on its way, go check your email" kind of page – usually called a "thank-you page". Space on this page normally is unused by most web sites.

You could use this space on the thank-you page to promote your own other lists, or to cross-promote the newsletter or web site of another publisher.

Co-registrations are very common among beginner or intermediate-level site publishers. Advanced publishers or site owners who are actually making money from their web sites, know the tremendous value of this thank-you page space, and will usually promote their own other sites, products, advertisements or affiliate links, and will not be willing to promote your product or service en gratis.

However, if you had a very powerful affiliate program, it will be a lot easier to persuade them to link to your product or service or newsletter using their affiliate link – of course, you would then be paying them for every visitor they send over to you – in the form of a percentage of the sale, or a flat fee per sale, or a flat fee per sign up (signing up for your list, that is).

Using Email Signatures

In the many years of my experience as a web-savvy internet user, I have seen a lot of people who post messages in forums or discussion lists with either of the following:

1. No signature at all

2. Not even a link to their web site

3. Absolutely no contact information or

4. They do post a signature, but with 'un-clickable' links

Not adding a signature is a missed opportunity to market your self or your site. For instance, whenever I read a post that makes sense to me, is just plain interesting or helps me learn something new, I would want to visit that person's web site to learn more about the person (or product) to see if I can learn something more from her web site or newsletter. So I usually look for a link at the end of the person's post.

And in many cases, there is none, or there is one but can't be clicked, and I would have to cut-n-paste into my browser) or I would have to decipher the domain name from the person's email address (if they have sent it from he@somesite.com instead of he@hotmail.com) and paste it into my browser - frankly, that's asking for too much!

Signatures are so important, that many smart Internet marketers look for any possible excuse just to post to a forum, just so that they can promote that new site or service through their signature.

Even though that is along the lines of spam, if you can post something meaningful that adds to the discussion thread, then most forums will let you get away with frequent posts.

So, make sure you add an 'interesting' signature to all your emails. Take the following example:

For a free subscription to my ezine,
send a blank message to
mailto:subscribe@NBLEB.com

The above signature is not bad, but not great either - it says nothing about you or your ezine to someone who doesn't already know you. There's nothing to excite someone into subscribing.

You need to develop a signature which will do one or more (or all) of the following:

- Invoke curiosity - Nothing creates a sense of urgency like curiosity can
- Shock, surprise, attract attention
- Make the reader pause, ponder, think, laugh or smile.

In fact, try and develop many different types of signatures, with differing themes (funny, curiosity-evoking, thought-provoking, free bonuses, discounted offers, sale announcements, one-time offers, etc) and rotate them frequently.

For instance, I have about 20 different signatures on my computer. Depending on whom I'm sending the email to, I use a different signature.

If it is a potential customer who is yet to buy from me, then I use a free bonus- or sale- related signature. In fact, I might even use a signature that I know is good at generating leads for my newsletter – because once they join my newsletter, I will be able to repeatedly market to them more effectively by sending content plus offers, rather than one-on-one email correspondence. While repeatedly corresponding with a prospect or subscriber, I even rotate the signatures just to keep it fresh.

In fact, these days I'm more aggressively promoting my blog RavisRants.com because RSS feeds are spam-filter proof, and are the ultimate opt-in vehicle to reach my subscribers (feed subscribers in this case, as against newsletter subscribers).

In the beginning, every time I wanted to change my email signature, I had to go to "My Documents", open up the "Signatures.txt" file, select one from a long list, come back to my email window and paste it into my email composition window. If you have Outlook Express 6, you have the option of selecting a signature right from the menu. But it still won't show you what each signature is before you select it.

But then I developed a piece of software called TypingAssistant (`VirtualTypingAssistant.com`) that can put the process of rotating email signatures on steroids.

I no longer need to use Eudora templates or Outlook express signatures. I have programmed the TypingAssistant software (a one-time task) with various keywords and the corresponding text for that keyword. This tool quietly sits in my desktop tray and monitors my keystroke combinations.

If I want signature 1, I just type in `rrsig` (short for "Ravi's Rants" Signature) and press "Enter". Gwala, the entire signature below appears in my email box like magic:

No Business Like E-Business – NBLEB.com

Ravi Jayagopal
For powerful SEO and Google Tips, visit
http://www.RavisRants.com

Things to think about when creating a Signature

1. Make your links clickable:
`LinkOverLoad.com` - wrong

(Most email clients won't show this as a 'clickable' link.)

www.LinkOverLoad.com - wrong again

(Some older email clients will still not show this as a link.)

`http://www.LinkOverLoad.com` - Right!

(All email clients will show it as a 'clickable' link)

2. Capitalizing your domain name to make it easy to read:

`http://www.linkoverload.com` - wrong

`http://www.Linkoverload.com` – ok, but can be better

`http://www.LinkOverLoad.com` – Perfect!

Note in the above example, how the case makes a difference to the link's readability.

3. Making your email addresses "clickable":

Ravi@WebmasterInABox.net – wrong, because most email clients won't show this as a 'clickable' link

`mailto:Ravi@WebmasterInABox.net` - right!

Adding a 'mailto:' in front of your email address makes it clickable when viewed in an email client. If you don't add this text, your subscriber has to copy-and-paste the email address into a new-email composition box just to send an email to the email id specified in your email..

Syndication and Reprint Rights

One way to market your newsletter is to allow other web site owners to re-print your entire newsletter, or a certain article you've written, in their own newsletter or on their site. This type of content syndication is a very popular way of getting free publicity, not to mention free incoming links to your web site – something that is extremely critical to gain higher PageRank.

Tracking Newsletter Performance

You should not just be tracking how many sales you get through sending out an offer in your newsletter, but you should also try to track how many people are actually reading your newsletters. There are many statistics you can track here:

- How many subscribers you have
- How many opened your email
- How many clicked on the first link versus the second link versus the last link, and so on.
- How many landed on your site and how many pages did they visit
- What were the entry and exit pages
- Did they go on to sign up for something, or did they go on to buy your product or service?

Some of the above are easier said than done. For example, one way in which you can track the "open rate" of your newsletter, is to send out what is called as a "web beacon" or a "web bug" in the HTML version of your newsletter. This is nothing but a invisible (or seemingly invisible) 1x1 pixel transparent gif image, embedded at the top or bottom of your newsletter's HTML code.

As you might have guessed already, there are many issues with this. Web-bugs will only work in the HTML versions of your newsletter, as the image will not be displayed in the text version. So, if you are publishing both text and HTML versions, then the "open rate" statistic has already become meaningless, because you cannot determine the open rate for your text-version subscribers.

Many email clients (like Gmail, Yahoo, and even desktop clients like Outlook and Outlook express) block such embedded images by default. Unless the reader agrees to enable the images in your newsletter, the web-bug will be blocked from being displayed. Which means the open-rate for even your HTML-version subscribers cannot be accurately determined.

Finally, even if the images are enabled, some email clients like Outlook show a "preview" of the email, which will trigger an impression of the 1x1 pixel image, but the reader may not really go on to read your actual email. So, you will be counting her as a subscriber who "opened" your email, but in reality her email client probably just showed her a preview and maybe she went on to delete it or put it away in some folder without ever even glancing at the contents. So, once again, this statistic is of no use.

Even though some may argue that 'no numbers' are better than 'incorrect numbers', I still feel that 'some numbers' are better than 'no numbers'. So go ahead and use web bugs, but use the results you get with caution.

Tracking Links

Tracking "click rate" in emails is extremely simple compared to tracking the "open rate". This is because link-tracking software makes it very easy to create unique links for each campaign or each volume of your newsletter, and in fact, you could even go on to create multiple tracking links for each link you have in your newsletter, even if they are all pointing to your main web site or blog.

But common sense and freely available research both point us to the fact that the very first link in an email is the one that gets clicked-on the most. So, make sure the first link is the link to your offer, or to your landing page to whatever it is that your "goal" is for that offer.

Also, sign up for the newsletters of successful Internet marketers like Stephen Pierce, Frank Kern and Mike Filsaime to see the way that they lead you to click on their links in their emails. Many times, there will not be any text that even says "click here". Instead, the copy of the email will be written in a way as to suggest that you need to click on the link provided, and the way the text will be worded, you will naturally tend to click on the link as you read through the email.

Tracking In-House and Third-Party Ads

One other metric you can track is the clicks on your links in third-party emails. This is especially helpful when you are doing a joint venture with another publisher, or doing paid-advertising by buying links in third-party newsletters. You should always try and track how many visitors your joint-venture (JV) partners are sending you – in fact, you could even track how many of *your* subscribers are clicking on your JV partners' links, so that you can exactly know how many clicks you sent them versus how many they sent you.

Also, if you are advertising on others' newsletters, then you still want to know how many clicks you got, and dividing that *into* the total cost, you will get to know exactly how much each click cost you.

This metric will be very useful in determining whether the ad campaign was a success or failure – because either way, you need to know whether to advertise more with this publisher, or to just stop because you know it didn't work.

Revenue from Newsletters

There are many ways to "monetizing" your emails/newsletters. Some are short-term, others long-term.

A long-term approach is the recommended one, because once you have someone for a long time on your list, over a period of time, you will be able to send them multiple offers for multiple products, and make money through both front-loaded as well as back-end offers.

Plus a large list will give you leverage with other successful publishers, and you can use this to do big-time joint ventures and gain access to a completely new target audience.

The short-term approach is to flood them with offers repeatedly, until they either buy from you, or get tired (or irritated) and drop off your list. This is not a very good way to build a long-lasting brand, but hey, this very approach says "short term" in its name!

There are many marketers who use short-term marketing with products or service which are not part of their main, long-term business. Many times, these marketers come up with new product ideas, and one way to quickly test if there's a market for the product is by doing short-term, throw-away campaigns, where you pay someone to quickly create an info-product, use a service like AdWords to get a flood of new visitors, and use a sign-up page to get their email address, and repeatedly send them emails 3 to 7 times a week (yup, almost every day!) till they either go on to purchase your product, or they just get fed-up of your spam, and unsubscribe from your list.

Big-dog marketers usually do all of this under aliases, and not under their real names, so their real brand doesn't get diluted because of the sneaky techniques they use in these kind of throw-away marketing strategies.

Marketing Your Own Product

Marketing your own product is probably the most profitable way to make money online, because as the owner of the product, you get to determine everything about the product – right from the sales page, to the pricing to the offers to the bonuses, customer service, etc.

This applies to you regardless of how you are marketing it – through a newsletter, or through a web site.

But if you are just starting out, it is easier to promote other people's products using an affiliate link to make sure you get a piece of the action (a flat fee per sale, or a percentage of the sale), because you don't have to worry about product creation, creating and optimizing the sales page, offering customer service and technical support, etc.

So, you could create newsletters along the lines of proven affiliate products, and then market these in your emails.

Or if you have your own product, you can market your own product in each email.

The key here is to balance the amount of *usable content* versus *sales pitch* in each of your emails. Too much or too little of either, and you can end up not making enough sales, or losing subscribers because they couldn't tolerate your marketing blitzes!

Finding Sponsors

Once your list gets substantially large (depending on the market, this could be 3,000 to 300,000), you will be able to attract individual and corporate sponsors for your emails.

This means, someone will pay you to publish a few lines of text along with a "trackable" link in your email, most of them wanting to see it at the top, and sometimes as part of your newsletter's actual content.

Affiliate Links

You can promote affiliate products closely related to the content of your newsletter. For example, if you are writing about "Home Improvement", then you can find a lot of related products – like furnishing, fittings, home décor, lawn and garden, do-it-yourself products, etc – that you can subtly promote by including them as part of your articles on that particular theme, or by doing product reviews or recommendations.

The bottom-line is to establish yourself as an expert in your domain, send out quality, useful and accurate information every time, and recommend quality products regardless of the commission you get paid, instead of recommending third-grade products that offer a high commission.

Integrity is paramount here, because if they know that you will only promote the best products, then your subscribers will click through your affiliate links, even if they know that those are affiliate links which will make you money.

However, there is a very fine line between being considered a greedy publisher who will promote anything for money, and a conscientious publisher who will promote products regardless of a revenue share in the sale, but will use affiliate links when available.

The only way to not cross the line into the realm of the "*pimp*ernet marketer" is to gain the trust of your subscribers first by sending out quality content, and by not pimping every info product that is being launched.

Joint Ventures

Why does Mike Tyson need a promoter? Mike, the undisputed Knock-Out King of Professional Boxing, earned about $400 million during his career , a big chunk of which went to Don King (and the lawyers, of course).

For someone who was as great as Iron Mike, why did he need someone else to promote him? Couldn't he have done it himself and saved about $200 million?

Michael Jordan did not win a championship until he learnt the importance of taking help from his phenomenal supporting cast of players led by Scottie Pippen.

Kobe Bryant of the L.A.Lakers, joined the ranks of Allen Iverson, Kevin Garnett and Tracy McGrady, when Shaq was traded to the Miami Heat, and found out the hard way, that individual glory means nothing without a championship ring.

Fortunately or unfortunately, that's the way the world works. "No man is an island", goes the saying. No one can do everything by themselves. Experts like Brian Tracy and Napoleon Hill call this "Masterminding". Others call it "Networking".

Either way, you need other people's help in order to succeed. For some, this person is someone from their own family - a devoted mother, or a passionate father (think *Williams Sisters*). The payoff for these people is seeing their children or protégé's succeed. Corporations rely on their executives and employees. And then the average person relies on his/her friends - or hires people who can help them fill in the blanks.

Without a support system, there would have been no Mike Tyson, no Williams sisters and no Michael Jordan.

In Internet marketing parlance, this support system is called a "Joint Venture" (JV). Put simply, this is a "You scratch my back, I scratch yours" arrangement.

In its simplest form, two e-Business owners get together and promote the other's products to their lists - I promote you to my mailing list, and you promote me to your mailing list. At the other end of the JV spectrum, big corporations recommend each other - like the now-sour Microsoft/AOL deal (Microsoft put an icon to the signup form for a new AOL account on every new computer sold that came pre-installed with some version of Windows ™, and in return AOL guaranteed that Microsoft's Internet Explorer is the default browser for all it's Internet Service users (ironical, since AOL owns Internet Explorer's arch nemesis, Netscape!).

You can see Joint Ventures in action every day.

Some JV's work by trading services for free, or almost-free, in exchange for future profits, while other JV's range from bartering free marketing services, to bartering millions of dollars worth of products and services.

Trial lawyers who are willing to help you sue a corporation or an individual for free, but will take a 50%-80% cut on the final settlement, which could run into millions of dollars if you have a valid case. Sales copy writers who will work for no fees, but will take a portion of your profits from all sales (regardless of whether they were generated by the ad in which you used their copy); or film stars who work for a pittance, but make sure they get a good chunk of the profits if the film succeeds (Sylvester Stallone in "Rocky", or Nia Vardalos in "My Big Fat Greek Wedding").

TV ads for a clinical product or drug, which has small text at the bottom of the ad that says "See our ad in so-and-so magazine". That's a JV right there between the product owner who paid for the ad, and the magazine owner - who made a small contribution towards the cost of buying that TV ad.

The merchants that Home Depot promotes the most are those that pay them the highest commissions - and in return, the merchants get heavy promotion - much more than their closest competitors. The same goes for eye-level and corner-of-aisle placements of products in your grocery store aisles.

Doctors in different fields promote each other - my children's Pediatrician has a ready list of referrals for surgeons, ENT specialists, Dermatologists, and other physicians in the area.

My car mechanic had the card of the tire store across the store quite handy, and even hurriedly wrote his name at the back. He specifically let me know to "ask for Mike" at the tire store - obviously, "Mike" must give him a nice little kickback (guessing anywhere between 1-10%) for every customer he sends over.

Joint Ventures are the easiest way to promote your product or service to a completely new audience. And it is also the easiest way to buy instant credibility and trust with people who have never heard about you before, just because the "host" of the show, or newsletter "publisher", or book "author" happened to recommend you.

This is why large corporations hire celebrity "spokespersons" for their brands, and sign them to extended contracts for long periods of time, so that the average consumer starts associating the celebrity with the product.

Would Nike ever have sold millions of pairs of sneakers - some even costing $150 - if it hadn't been for those mind-blowing, slow motion images of "His Airness" Jordan with his classic high-flying one-handed "Jumpman" dunk?

Some of the celebrities who are closely associated with the product they promote are:

- Michael Jordan & Nike.
- Bob Vila and the Home Improvement show
- William Shatner & Priceline.com
- Sachin Tendulkar (Indian cricketer) and Pepsi

- Kobe Bryant and Sprite
- James Earl Jones and Verizon

Remember, the borrowed credibility you get, is only as good as the credibility of the person recommending you. Is it then any wonder why McDonald's and a slew of other sponsors dropped Kobe from their ad campaigns soon after the rape accusation?

If Kobe is tainted, then the products he recommends will also be seen as tainted by the public. No company wants that. They'd rather not advertise at all, than get associated with any kind of negativity.

Fortunately for Kobe, public memory is short. If he spends a few years lying low, slowly gaining back the "clean" reputation he once had, and continues to win championships, it won't be long before these same companies go back to him. It may never be the same again for him from the perspective of his public image or the way his family and friends view him, but the advertisers? Oh, they will certainly be back.

14. Converting Visitors into Customers

WIIFM (What's In It For "Me")

When was the last time you wanted to buy a car, got all pumped up and excited about it, got ready to buy, went to a car dealer, and asked the salesman, "What's in it for me"?

The theory of establishing what purchasing a product will do for a potential customer is all well and good when listening to so called "powerful" Internet marketing seminars and how-to books.

If your product can solve someone's problem, and you are able to get that person to your web site and do a reasonable job of conveying how your product will solve your visitor's problem, then you don't need to have 50 bullet points in your sales letter.

If your product is abstract, your sales pitch is not obvious, and you are trying to increase the "perceived" value of a mediocre product, then you better start writing essays about all the benefits and the features. You still may not sell any products, but at least you would have made an honest attempt to list everything you could conceivably list about your product.

Corleone-Marketing

"I'm gonna make him an offer he can't refuse".

Those were the words of the Don *Vito Corleone* in one of the greatest movies of all time, "The Godfather".

Marketing gurus like Jay Abraham will tell you that you've got to overwhelm your prospects with such an irresistible offer, that there is no possible way of your prospect saying "no".

It is about removing all possible objections to the sale.

Objection: "I don't know if it will fit me"
Response: "Go ahead and try it – there's a changing room at the back"

Objection: "What if I feel later that it doesn't really suit me?"
Response: "Take it home and try it – as long as you don't damage it, you can always return it within 30 days for a full refund."

Objection: "What if I am paying too much?"
Response #1: "If you find someone else selling it for less, let us know and we'll refund the difference."
Response #2 (better): "We'll not only refund the difference, we'll even give you an extra $10 cash-back if you find a lower price elsewhere".

Objection: "What if it breaks in a few months"?
Response: "You have a one-year guarantee/warranty".

Objection: "Let me think about it".
Response: "If you buy now, you'll not only get 25% discount, but you'll also get all these fabulous free bonuses - yours to keep even if you decide to return the product. Oh, by the way, this offer ends tomorrow".

You get the idea.

Incentives Don't Always Make the Sale

Here's a point of view directly contradictory to the previous section, but I need to tell you about it any way.

My flagship site `WebmasterInABox.net` was born out of my own need to solve my programming needs. As a small e-business owner, if I had those problems, I was willing to bet that most people in my category would have similar problems.

If my scripts helped solve my problems, I was sure it would help solve theirs too. After all, every business web site needs programming. You cannot expect to sell simply by posting a huge PDF document on your site. So, the "need" for my product was first established.

The demographics of my potential customers were clear – small e-business owners with a web site who needed to add programming to their site in an affordable way.

Now, these folks had a choice – they could either hire someone to build it all from scratch, while assuming the risk of not knowing whether the end product would be exactly what they wanted – or they could purchasing my product for a lot fewer dollars.

In spite of having a "sellable" product, I still needed to persuade visitors to "buy now". To do so, I have offered tons of incentives over the years – to not just my site visitors, but even to other fellow site owners to recommend my products to their visitors and newsletter subscribers.

I have found that the absolute best incentive for a visitor to buy your product online, right then and there during their first visit to your site, is to have a really awesome product that solves exactly the problem that they may be having – and to make it absolutely clear to them in every possible way, that it is indeed the answer to their problem.

Of course, you would still have to present it to the right audience, the right way. It doesn't matter if you have the greatest online shoe store – I would never respond to your ads, I would never search for a shoe store online, I would never stick around on your site (even assuming I was tricked into coming there by a sly popup ad), let alone purchase anything from your site.

The key is to not only have a great product, but to make sure you are presenting it to those who actually need (or want) it – people who are actually looking to buy your product – people who are walking around with a credit card in their hand, willing to dish it out to the first person who will help them solve that nagging, urgent, irritating, bothersome, painful problem that they are having.

Establishing Trust

For a complete stranger who has never seen you, and probably may never do so, to purchase your product, the major factor is trust.

They need to be able to trust you, understand that you are expert on your subject, that you are an authority in your industry, that you know what you are talking about, and that your product will really solve their problem.

There are many ways to establish credibility – which in turn increases your trust-worthiness:

Hiring a famous spokesperson (borrowed credibility)

If you are like me, then you can't afford to pay someone, or to create and broadcast TV or radio advertisements. If you are starting out, you most definitely should not even think about this option.

Doing Joint Ventures (borrowed credibility)

You could work with well-respected e-Business owners, or well-established list owners – obviously offering them a substantial chunk of the profits from the sales they send your way, in return.

The credibility established in the audience of your joint venture partner, will only be as good as the partner's own. So, be very careful in choosing your partners. Joint ventures are still much cheaper and probably a lot more powerful (in terms of money spent vs. credibility gained) than simply hiring a paid spokesperson that would have never used your product if not for that check you wrote them).

Allowing your current clients to promote you

Allow your existing customers – and possibly fellow site owners – to promote your product – once again, in return for a portion of the profits, or even per visitor sent.

This is a very powerful way of increasing exposure, because you are giving your customers – who have paid for and used your product extensively in some cases – a tool to recommend your product to their associates and their audience.

And if you have a great product with really ecstatic users, you are just giving them an additional incentive to share their excitement and enthusiasm about your product, with their audience.

Seth Godin calls this "Flipping the funnel". Instead of the usual upright "sales funnel" with the narrow end at the bottom (which is how a potential customer arrives at your web site and moves through the sales cycle, coming out at the bottom as customer), if you flipped the funnel 90", it then becomes a "mega phone", which is the symbolic empowerment of your customers to promote you (by "announcing you over the mega phone") to their family, friends and colleagues.

Develop content

Probably the most powerful way to prove that you know what you are talking about, publishing lots of helpful content in which you share your "expertise", "experience" and "wisdom" and offer "tips", "tricks" and "guidance" and "answer questions" is an almost guaranteed way to achieve success.

This might seem like an obvious thing to do, but if you pay attention to the various small e-Business web sites you visit, you will see that the obvious is not being done.

Show proof that your product works

Publishing emails or letters (a.k.a. testimonials) from actual customers is a very powerful way to establish trust. And if these people are real (maybe they are quite well known in your industry, or you have published their web site name, instead of simply writing "Here's an email from Mary, New York". Mary who? Peter what? How do I know these are real?), it adds to the authenticity of your testimonials and makes you look legitimate.

You may have seen those late night direct marketing ads for weight-loss, financial or real estate products. Every good ad without exception features actual people – real consumers – who talk about their personal experience with their product.

It is another story that they may have been paid to do so (but why should any one do it for free, when the merchant is going to be using their testimonial to make more money? It's not like it the merchant id doing it for charity).

Paid or not, staged or not, these are actual customers who have used the product, and they even have "before" and "after" pictures to prove it.

Ads for financial products may feature images of actual checks or receipts or other proof of income to show that the product actually makes you money.

It is also a common practice in direct-marketing web sites to provide audio clips of customers' voice mail (of course, you could legitimately request them to leave you one – maybe even offer them a nice incentive – such as cash, discount, free products - to do so).

Using Follow-up Software

Imagine keeping track of how many times you emailed each of your thousands of subscribers, and when you last emailed them so that you don't send them too many too soon.

That would be a full time job in itself, won't it? The good news is that there is software available that lets you "pre-schedule" all of the email follow ups to be sent to your customers or subscribers, all at pre-set intervals chosen so as to not be too aggressive, yet not too far apart from each other.

This kind of a pre-scheduled email list is generally dubbed as "Sequential Autoresponders" – meaning, these lists send subscribers an autoresponse (no manual sending required – just like your out-of-office autoreply at work) in a sequential fashion to completely automate your follow ups.

So, for instance, you could set up your autoresponder to send out emails on day 1, day 3, day 7, 21 and so on. Or you can program it to send one every Monday (say) if you are publishing a weekly e-newsletter.

15. Referral Marketing

Referral marketing is about getting people who have used or purchased your product to refer their associates, friends or family to you.

This is the cheapest, and arguably the most powerful form of marketing. Jay Abraham, in his book "**Getting everything out of all you've got - 21 Ways You Can Out-Think, Out-Perform, and Out-Earn the Competition**", lists referral marketing as one of the absolutely must-do things on any business owner's to-do list.

If you break down the goals of any business, it comes down to these five things:

Product development: Creating a brilliant product or service

Lead generation: Generating a flow of potential customers

Conversion: Converting those leads to buy from you

Customer Retention: Keeping your existing customers happy, and preventing them from switching to your competitors by continuously improving your product, adding more features and improving user experience.

Referral marketing: Getting them to refer more customers – in the orm of their associates, friends or family - this can be further broken down into three different types: Recommendation marketing, Viral marketing and Affiliate Marketing

Recommendation Marketing

Recommendation marketing is at work when people casually recommend you to others when their friends or family ask them specifically for recommendations about the industry they are in.

This can happen in different ways: For instance, a friend expresses dissatisfaction about a similar product that she is using – and if your customer is happy with your product, he will recommend your product to his friend.

Friend: "Had a lousy day today. Ended up spending most of my day at the doctor's. They are too far from where I live, and their wait times are ridiculous – and their timings are very inconvenient"

Your Customer: "Hey, you should think about going to my doctor. They are not very close either, but they are open early and late. And they work half a day on Saturdays too. And they have multiple doctor's – so the wait is usually not bad at all."

Friend: "Hey, do you know of a good place to eat? I want to take my girlfriend out this weekend".

Your Customer: "You should check out Joe's Restaurant. I was there last week. Their food is really amazing, and they have a really nice ambience – nice lighting, pretty good service and reasonable prices too."

In both the examples above, it was the friend who initiated the referral, by asking for a recommendation. Recommendation marketing is good for the long term. It takes time to work, simply because it is not every day that people are asking their friends for recommendations about products or services they use. Plus, there is no real incentive for your customers to actually go out and tell their friends about you.

However, this very fact that your customers have no incentive to talk about you makes this a very powerful form of marketing. When people know that their friends are not getting paid to recommend someone or something, the level of trust is at its highest, and the chances of this new lead (the friend) converting (becoming your customer) are extremely high.

Incentive-Based Recommendation Marketing

You could add a little vigor to this laid back recommendation marketing – by putting a little spin on it: Offering an incentive to your customers for referring others to you.

Now this incentive could be something as simple as gratification – that feeling of "I told you first" which is what drives **Viral Marketing**.

Or this incentive could be monetary – or materialistic – which is referred to as **Affiliate Marketing**. For instance, you could share with your customer, a percentage of the profits from the friend's purchase. Or you could give your customer a discount on their next purchase – or say, give them a month's service (or supply) for free.

Viral Marketing

This is referral marketing on steroids.

In this form, people don't just recommend your product to their friends and services; they become a voluntary, unpaid, sales representative for your company – and literally go to the extent of selling your product to everyone they know – and their mother – and her dog.

These folks are so excited about your product that they send emails to everyone they know – about how awesome your product is, how much better their life is because of it – and how no one should ever buy anything else but your product.

Your marketing campaign spreads like a virus – from one person to another – at the speed of light – without you having to spend a dime. These "evangelists" take it upon themselves to make the lives of all their friends and family better, by persuading them to buy or use your product, all by themselves.

It is every marketer's dream to create a campaign so viral, that the ROI – Return on Investment – goes through the roof. Spend $x and get back $100x in return, is what every company fantasizes about.

Customers are the life-blood of any organization. To get customers, you need leads – and you need to be able to convert those leads.

Great marketing can sell a mediocre or sometimes even a lousy product.

Lousy marketing cannot sell a great product.

There is a caveat to the "Lousy marketing/Great product" scenario – your product can still be a success with poor marketing if your product is something that large numbers of people need – and this need is not already satisfactorily fulfilled.

Apple's Macintosh immediately comes to mind (the Apple of the olden days). Apple lost a crippling number of computer users to Microsoft, but there is a certain pride that comes with being the owner of a PowerBook – that will never be experienced by Microsoft's users.

Apple was the one who invented the concept of a Mouse-driven Graphical User Interface (GUI). And the Mac User Interface beats the Windows GUI hands down, any day.

But Apple did not part with the OS. They said, if you want to use our Operating System, you've got to buy our computers, which by the way can be made only by us. They completely locked out the third-parties.

But Microsoft had a better marketing plan. They not only created comparable software, but they mass marketed it. They not only made it inexpensive enough for the average person to afford it, but also made it available for any computer hardware manufacturer to sell it pre-installed on the computer.

This meant that the hardware giants like IBM and Dell did not have to worry about the operating system – all they had to do was install Windows on the computers that they were selling. Now, they were not only able to sell more computers, but they also got price breaks if they exclusive installed Windows on all their shipped computers.

More people buying Windows based computers, meant more third-party software vendors scrambling to create software and hardware compatible exclusively with Microsoft Windows, ignoring the relatively small percentage of users of other operating systems (like Apple's Mac OS).

This became a vicious cycle that Apple could never get out of.

This ultimately meant that buying Windows made the most business and financial sense for customers. And for the most part, they were ready to put up with the bugs, the glitches, the poor user experience, the lousy performance and the incessant crashes (widely known as "The Blue Screen of Death").

This endless-loop marketing strategy from Microsoft was hard to beat. And it continues to be a huge challenge even to this day.

16. Affiliate Marketing

One of the ways to get people to recommend your product and send you leads, is through *Affiliate Marketing*.

An "affiliate" in the online world (even though the word is applicable in the off-line world) is simply one who owns a web site or an e-Business, who is willing to promote your product on their web site to their visitors, newsletter subscribers, and customers, using a "special" link.

When their referrals click on this link and arrive at your web site, using programming, a special kind of tracking code, called a "cookie" is set on the lead's computer.

If this lead either goes on to purchase your product right away (which is highly unlikely to happen as this is her very first visit), or if she bookmarks your site or even memorizes your web site link only to return later – be it a few hours, or a few days, or even a few months later – your affiliate who originally "referred" this lead to your web site, will automatically get a percentage of your profits.

Of course, you determine what this percentage is, and you and your affiliate both have to use a pre-determined, common way of tracking leads and purchases.

The Advantages of Affiliate Marketing

Paying Only for Performance

The most obvious advantage is that you are getting a voluntary, non-salaried, sales representative who is willing to promote your product for just a portion of the profits. You are not paying your affiliates up-front. You pay them only when there is a sale – that is, only if the lead they send you goes on to purchase your product, or signs up

If this lead does not ever purchase your product, neither of you make any money.

It is a win-win situation for you. You don't part with a cent until you make some yourself. If you make money, they make money too. If you don't, they don't either.

You can extend this concept further, and pay your affiliates not just on sales, but even on other types of results – say, paying per lead. You could pay your affiliates for every visitor they send you, who signs up for your newsletter; for every time they fill out a survey, for filling out a form, for signing up for a promotion, signing up for a trial, and so on.

Once again, the point is, you are still paying only based on performance – or results – not up front.

Link Popularity

Link Popularity is one of the ways in which some search engines decide how high you come up in search results.

Your site's *link popularity* is roughly calculated based on the number of web sites that link to your web site, from any page on their web site. It certainly helps your link popularity, if the sites linking to you, have a high link popularity rating themselves.

When you have hundreds of affiliates linking to your site, regardless of the motivation behind the linking, it still helps your link popularity. This means, in a search for a particular set of keywords, your web site has a better chance of appearing on the first few pages of the search, rather than further below.

And using search engine optimization techniques, you can further fine tune your web site content such that your site appears among the top 5 results of a search.

See the chapter "Search Engine Optimization" for more affiliate link related tips and strategies.

Disadvantages of Affiliate Marketing

Affiliate marketing is not as simple as it seems.

High Sweat Equity for Your Affiliate

Let's say you pay your affiliates only per sale. Now, this works wonderfully well in your favor, but works against your affiliates.

Your affiliates may have to end up sending hundreds or even thousands of referrals to your site before they can make any money. This is not a very encouraging factor, and most affiliates drop out of their programs in the first month if they don't see results.

So, it is very important for you to monitor your lead-to-sale conversion ratio, and continue to improve your content and sales copy to make sure a higher percentage of people who land at your site, go on to purchasing your product.

Less Control over Referrals for the Affiliate

Your affiliates are depending on your capability to convert the visitors they send your way, into customers. They have very little control over the whole process, but for using their special tracking link and waiting for some one to click on the link, and hoping that they go on to purchase something from you.

It takes a lot of tact, marketing skills, and large doses of patience on both sides (you and your affiliate) to make affiliate marketing a success.

Potential Loss of Credit for the Affiliate

Affiliate programs rely on technology – the ability of a computer program to place a cookie on the referral's computer – to track the sale.

If for some reason this cookie cannot be set on the referral's computer, then there is no way for your shopping cart program to recognize who exactly sent you this referral. Which means, even if this lead goes on to purchase your product, the affiliate will never get the credit for the sale.

This loss of credit could also happen if you have multiple channels of sales – for instance, the ability for visitors to order by phone. You could not possibly track this "cookie" information if you are taking orders by phone. The cookies work only if the orders are placed online. This means, you still get the sale, and your affiliate doesn't get any share from the profits, because you did not have a better way of tracking affiliates in the case of phone orders.

Sure it's a win/win proposition for you, but lose/lose for your affiliate, who not only lost all that time in promoting your product, all that effort, but lost that all-important sale too, simply because you didn't have a proper process in place to give them the credit they deserved.

High Maintenance

Even though you pay them, your affiliates are more like partners than employees.

You need to treat them with respect, and constantly provide them with tools and information in order to sell better.

They can promote your competitor's products just as easily as they promote yours. Of course, we are not talking about the bottom-dwelling, greedy-for-cash site owners who will switch from vendor to vendor if only they paid them a few cents more in commissions.

For example, take web hosting. I have seen 5-10 ads for web hosting on the same page of many web sites. These folks have a page full of flashing ads thinking the more the number of ads, the chances of the visitor clicking on at least one of them is much higher.

It is the same mentality as a spammer. Spammers send out millions of emails with the hope that if even a fraction of one percent of the recipients buy something from links in the email, even that is a profit return of more than a thousand times over, as they probably didn't spend even one red cent sending out the spam.

You need to separate the spammers from the real guys. And you need to try and work with them one-on-one.

You have to be accessible to them if they have any questions. You need to reply to their emails within a reasonable amount of time. You should encourage the high-performers with better commission rates, special offers and other cash incentives.

You need to send them their checks on time as promised.

The minimum amount for checks to be sent, should kept reasonably low. I have been a part of affiliate programs (as an affiliate myself) that expect you to accrue at least $100 in commissions before they pay you even one cent.

Reporting.net was one such affiliate service provider, where merchants got to set their own individual minimums before affiliates can get paid. This is usually $25 as I have seen.

So if you promote Merchants M1, M2 and M3 aggressively for months, and manage to accumulate $10 in commissions from each merchant, you have basically accumulated a total of $30 in commissions, which is technically more than the $25-minimum that you need to get a payout.

But guess what? You won't see one red cent from any of these three merchants unless your total reaches their specified minimum of $25 *per merchant* before you get paid *anything*.

So, even if you promoted these guys heavily for a whole year, and manage to earn $24.99 per merchant, and a total of $74.97 in commissions, you *still* won't see one red cent because you still haven't reached the $25 minimum for an individual merchant.

And during all that time, these merchants have been enjoying those thousands of visitors from your promotions.

Some visitors obviously went on to purchase something from these merchants, which resulted in the commissions in your account. But it is a high likelihood that many of them completed their purchase from a computer other than the one that they were using when they actually clicked on your affiliate link.

The tracking cookie was set on one computer, but the sale was made from another. This means that you never got credit for that sale. Quite possibly, you never received credit for tens or hundreds of your referrals.

The merchant still made all that money thanks to you, not to mention all those future, back-end repeat sales to these customers, for which they are not going to pay you any commissions anyway. So, in the end, you end up losing, while the merchant almost always wins.

Making Your Affiliate Marketing Strategy a Success

As the merchant, you play a substantial role in the success of your affiliates. Here are a few things you could do to improve their sales, and consequently, your own bottom-line.

Establish a Relationship

Relationships are the key here. You need to be able to establish a one-on-one, first name basis, relationship with your affiliates. It may be hard to do if you have thousands of affiliates, but it still needs to be done.

It is important for your affiliate to know that they matter to you – that they are not "just another email address on your bulk mail list"; that you are willing to answer questions reasonably quickly, that you are flexible in your performance terms for the high performers.

Training and Guidance

Provide them with training and guidance– not just terms and conditions. You are supposed to be the authority with regards to your product – and the target market. You need to be aware and up to date on the current trends, marketing strategies, sales copy writing techniques, and industry preferences, and timing.

Provide them with ready-to-use sales copy, email and newsletter templates, customizable HTML pages with graphics, referral and recommendation techniques that you are tried and tested, and tips and tricks to help them prepare their lead better before they arrive at your site.

It is called "Pre-Selling", a word made famous in the online world of affiliates, by Dr. Ken Evoy of SiteSell.com.

What I Recommend

If you want to join affiliate programs and make money recommending other people's products and services, then the affiliate service providers I that I highly recommend are:

- `CommissionJunction.com`
- `ClickBank.com`
- `LinkShare.com`
- `Amazon.com`
- `Google Referrals (part of Adsense)`

I recommend them due to their vast reach in terms of the number of merchants who are running promotions through them, and their attractive business model where commissions from different vendors can be rolled up into one account, which means you reach your minimum-payment-amount faster, and you will get paid faster.

Also, CommissionJunction and Amazon offer direct deposit – which means you don't have to wait for the check in the mail, but can have it directly deposited into your bank account automatically.

Google referrals launched recently at the time of writing this book, and is available through your AdSense account (when you log in to your account, you will see the "Referrals" link under the "AdSense Setup" tab). I haven't used it much yet, as it is still in its early stages and doesn't have many merchants on-board, but I'm predicting it will be the one to watch out for, as Google signs up more merchants, offers more tools to the publisher, and integrates its various services (like referrals, Analytics, AdWords, radio ads, video ads etc).

17. Tips, Tricks and Hacks

This section lists some of the less commonly known tricks and hacks, that you can use to not just be more productive, but also to arm yourself with some very powerful information about your site – and most importantly, about your competitors' sites – that you can then use to improve your site, your PageRank, and eventually, your traffic.

Productivity and Time Management

As you start publishing your web site, create products and start selling online, you will discover that you need to perform a range of tasks on a daily basis.

And if you are like me, then you have a full-time day job, kids, family and household chores to take care of. This means that as you understand more and start doing more, you will realize that you will have lesser and lesser time to do all of them.

There are only so many things you can give up. For instance, as I continued to grow my ebusiness, I gave up all of the following:

- Watching TV/movies/sports (cut it down to one movie a weekend)
- Reading fiction/magazines

- Sleeping 8 hours a night (cut it down to 6)
- Hanging out with friends for hours (became an occasional quick call while driving the kids somewhere)
- Watching the news (gave way to Digg'ing and RSS feeds)
- Listening to music (gave way to tech and how-to podcasts)

And the number of things I eventually gave up was too many and too trivial to list here. But you get the idea.

There are only so many things you can sacrifice, before you realize that you've cut right down to the bones, and then there's only one way to do more with less time – that is to work smart and utilize tools, technology and outsourcing to take some of the load off your back.

Knowing *how to type* will be one of the biggest factors in your success. Can't type, can't win. This is so obvious, but not many get it, and try to get by with just poking at the keyboard with a few fingers.

Knowing your way around the keyboard – especially in the form of keyboard shortcuts - will also help you save time, big time!

But first, it all starts with your browser. I recommend using FireFox as your primary browser, and forgetting Internet Explorer. FireFox, being open-source, has a large community of people who have developed (and will continue to develop) add-on software for your browser, which make a lot of common tasks as simple as clicking your mouse button. I cannot even begin to tell you how many tens-, if not hundreds-, of hours I save each month simply by using a variety of FireFox plugins and add-ons. My favorite ones are listed further below.

Keyboard Shortcuts

For General Typing

Ctrl+Turning Mouse Wheel: Turning the wheel up will enlarge the text size on most applications, including browser windows. Turning the wheel down will decrease the text size.

Ctrl+Backspace: Delete the entire previous word from cursor position

Ctrl+W: Close (active window or application)

Ctrl+Q: Quit

Ctrl+Z: Undo

Ctrl+Y: Redo

Ctrl+C: Copy

Ctrl+X: Cut

Ctrl+V: Paste

Ctrl+B: Bold

Ctrl+I: Italics

Ctrl+O: Open

Depending on which software you use, there will be more shortcuts available to you.

Browser Shortcuts

Ctrl+T: Open a new tab

Ctrl+N: New browser window

Ctrl+L: Highlight browser location (where you type in the site name)

Ctrl+W: Close active browser window (or tab)

Ctrl+Shift+esc: Bring up the Task Manager

Ctrl+Click & Shift+Click:

These are my personal favorites: When you hold down the "Ctrl" key as you click on a link, it will open in a new tab within the same browser window. And if you hold down the "Shift" key while clicking on a link, the link will open in an entirely new browser window.

You can use Ctrl+Click to open related links within the same browser window, but on different tabs, so you can do this for logically related content (for eg., when you are doing a search, use Ctrl+Click to open up the various search results in different tabs, but within the same browser window).

This will save you a lot of time, as you won't have to keep hitting the "back" button when searching for information and browsing through a lot of sites, just to figure out where you were.

Even while checking email, you can use Ctrl+Click to open up the various emails from your inbox in various tabs within the same window, and use "Shift+Click" to open up any links within those emails in an entirely new browser window. These two little browsing tricks alone will save you tons of time.

You can press "Ctrl+W" to close an entire browser window (if it doesn't have any tabs) or if it has multiple tabs, it will close the tab that you are currently on.

In fact, if you do a lot of Googling, then you can even set your Google preferences (on the home page, click on the small "preferences" link next to the search box, scroll down and check the **Results Window** checkbox to open search results in a new browser window).

Another browsing trick is to hit the spacebar to make the page scroll down. Very useful when trying to sit back and read through a long web page – when you want to scroll down, you don't have to look for either the "Page down" key or the mouse.

Google Hacks

Perform the relevant searches shown below on all of your competitors' web sites and compare them to your own site's results. That will prove to be a good exercise in understanding why your competitor's rank they way they do.

```
link:Example.com
```

This query is used to search for all incoming links to Example.com. MSN and Yahoo display the most number of incoming links, while Google has officially acknowledged that it displays only a subset of all incoming links. So, check Google, Yahoo and MSN for incoming links if you really want a true, all-inclusive count.

```
site:Example.com
```

This query shows the number of pages in your web site as indexed by Google. So, if you just added a new page, it may not show up on this list. One of the key to improving your PageRank is to increase the number shown on this list.

```
info:Example.com
```

This query will show what Google knows about your site, which includes a link to your main page, followed by a description (usually the meta tag "description"). If you don't see any information, then your site is quite possibly in the supplemental index, either about to be included in the main index, or about to be de-listed from Google altogether.

```
allintitle:php scripts
```

This query will restrict the search to those pages that have all of the query words - "php" and "scripts" in this example - in the page title (HTML <title> tag).

```
allinurl:indian baby names
```

This query shows all web pages that contain the words "Indian", "baby" and "names" in the URL – includes both the domain name and the page name.

Using Double Quotes:

When you enclose your search keywords within double quotes – like searching for *"firefox tips"* (typing in the quotes too into the search box) instead of just *firefox tips*, then you are searching for web pages with the exact string "firefox tips", in that same order. So, if a web page had the text "firefox tricks" and "tips on using firefox" in different parts of the page, it won't show up during this specific search.

Using the "-" for exclusion: You can exclude keywords (and even entire web sites) from your search when you add the "-" in front of a keyword. Example:

```
hardware stores -computer
```

Here, you are searching for web pages with the words *hardware* and the word *stores*, not necessarily together (because you didn't enclose the search string in double quotes, remember?), but pages which don't want contain the word *computer*, because you don't want computer hardware to be included in your search results.

Using the "+" for inclusion:

You can make a keyword mandatory by including the "+" in front of it. Example:

`computer software +free`

Here you are searching for the words *computer* and *software*, in any order, anywhere on a page, but the page must also have the word *free*.

Combination Searches

Keywords + "site:" search:

When you want to search only a specific site, you can add the "site:" tag to your search. Example:

`Clickbank site:MyWebmasterInABox.com`

Here, you are searching for the word `ClickBank` only within the site `MyWebmasterInABox.com`

"link:" and "site:":

Example:

link:RavisRants.com –site:RavisRants.com

Here, you are searching for all links to RavisRants.com, but excluding links from the site itself.

For more such tips on advanced search, go to:

`Google.com/help/refinesearch.html`

FireFox Plugins

My favorite Firefox plugins are:

Google Toolbar: `Google.com/tools/firefox/toolbar/`

You can search without having to go to Google.com, plus other Google goodies like PageRank, Info, etc.

IE Tab: `ietab.mozdev.org`

Lets you embed Internet Explorer in a Mozilla/Firefox tab so that you can preview what your pages look like in IE right from within Firefox, without having to open up IE.

Down Them All: `downthemall.net`

Lets you download all the links or images contained in a webpage

GreaseMonkey: `greasemonkey.mozdev.org`

Lets you to add bits of "user scripts" to any web page to change its default behavior. For example, to make all URLs displayed in the browser are clickable links (even if the web page itself shows it just as plain text, and not as a link)

WebDeveloper: `chrispederick.com/work/webdeveloper`

A very handy web master/web developer plugin with a lot of commonly used tools (view session variables, disable javascript, etc).

StumbleUpon.com: Discover cool new sites based on your preferences.

Del.icio.us.com: For storing and sharing your bookmarks online

ColorZilla: `iosart.com/firefox/colorzilla`

ColorPicker, Eyedropper, Page Zoomer and other goodies.

Aardvark: `karmatics.com/aardvark`

Clean up unwanted banners and surrounding "fluff," especially prior to printing a page, see how the page is created, block by block

Google Extension for Firefox: `tools.google.com/firefox`

Check out and download other Google extensions here – including the Google toolbar and Google notebook extension.

18. Marketing with RSS Feeds

What is RSS?

RSS primarily stands for *Really Simple Syndication* (and depending on which version of RSS you are referring to, could also stand for *Rich Site Summary* or *RDF Site Summary*).

Put simply, think of it as a way to receive or publish content without using email.

Strip away all the "styling" elements of a web page – like bold, italics, fonts, tables – and what is left behind is pure content. Imagine sending just the pure content of news items – like headline, body and link – to your subscribers, and allowing them to format it and view it in any way or on any device they choose. This bare-bones, content-only document is your RSS feed.

When you give people the power of receiving just your content, they can then choose to consume it in a variety of formats – using their favorite "feed reader" desktop software, or online feed aggregators like Google reader (Google.com/reader), LinkOverLoad.com or BlogLines.com, or they can mix-and-match feeds and create their own mashups, or even publish your feeds on their site.

In 2005-2006, RSS finally graduated from being three-lettered geek-speak to common-man territory. Thanks to an explosion in RSS/Atom/XML based content aggregator sites and, the popularity of RSS feed syndication rose to the extent that feeds were both abused by spammers, as well as entire commercial sites and services were built around feeds, like FeedBurner.com.

Another main factor for this was the availability of free, easy to use, powerful feed-publishing software like Magpie RSS, which let anyone publish any feed in real time within minutes on their web pages.

RSS vs. Email

In the beginning, RSS was considered advantageous over Email because of *delivery*-related factors. For instance, email could be "lost" or end up in the "spam" folder for a variety of reasons, including spam filters deployed by the email service provider or ISP. Email also runs the risk of getting wrongly reported as spam, and could get your site and even your domain name suspended.

Whereas, RSS guarantees delivery of your message to whoever subscribes to your RSS feed. As long as they have internet access, and your RSS feed is available and your web site up-and-running, they can access your RSS feed using either desktop-based or web-based feed readers. There are no filters or ISP's or spam issues to deal with when it comes to RSS.

Initially, one of the main disadvantages of RSS was bandwidth usage – every time someone fired up their feed reader, depending on how their reader was configured, your RSS feed (which is nothing but a file on your web site) could be downloaded potentially hundreds or thousands of times a day. This meant huge bandwidth costs and high usage of your web site's server resources.

But in the last few years, hosting has become so competitive and inexpensive, that bandwidth and resources are no longer a constraint. In fact, you can get your own high-powered server with unlimited bandwidth for under $100 per month – 5 years ago, this price was unheard of, and the same server would have cost about $5000.

However, as RSS has matured and the power of the web has shifted towards a "pull" flavor (where web users pull, aggregate and consume content from a variety of sources online) instead of "push" (where you push content onto users – like email, broadcasting content onto desktops, etc)

Feed Formats

It doesn't really matter what format the feeds are. They are becoming universally accepted, and lots of web applications have built-in support for them. So you don't really need to worry about this. So, feel free to skip to the next section ("Creating Your Own Feed").

Feeds come in many flavors. This is due to introduction of new XML formats, as standards were improved upon and diverged from the original specification. So, we are now left with the following formats:

- RSS 0.90, 0.91, 0.92, 0.93, 0.94, 1.0, 1.1, 2.0
- Atom

Atom was popularized primarily by Google when their Blogger.com service started publishing Atom feeds by default.

If you must, you can read more about Atom and RSS by visiting:

- `Webreference.com/authoring/languages/xml/rss/`
- `xml.com/pub/a/2002/12/18/dive-into-xml.html`
- `en.wikipedia.org/wiki/RSS_(file_format)`
- `AtomEnabled.org/`
- `en.wikipedia.org/wiki/Atom`
- `IETF.org/rfc/rfc4287`

WordPress by default supports RSS 0.92, 1.0, 2.0 and Atom. Google recommends both RSS 2.0 and Atom. So, you would be fine supporting just the common denominator of RSS 2.0 and Atom. All you need to do is to publish one or the other – not both – because most feed readers can handle multiple feed formats.

Creating Your Own Feed

If you use industry-standard blog software like WordPress or Blogger, then the software itself creates the RSS feed for you. In fact, the software creates a blog-wide main feed, feeds for individual posts, and one even for the comments section.

You will still need to highlight the link to your feed on your blog because the default link and placement of the link that comes out of the box with the blog software, is very subtle and not visible.

You can do this by adding your own images for your feed, and linking it to the actual feed, or you can use free services like AddThis.com or FeedButton.com that give you free images along with the HTML code that lets your users not just subscribe to your feed, but also bookmark it and add it to high-traffic social networking sites like Digg.com, Reddit.com, Furl.com and Netscape.com.

You can also create your own feed manually, using free sites like `FeedYes.com` or `Feed43.com`, but it is recommended that you let your blog software handle this, as that will make the process painless and fully automated.

Promoting Your RSS Feed

Promoting your feed is very similar to promoting your newsletter – there are no shortcuts.

It is all about creating quality content, and driving traffic to your blog, and giving people the need to subscribe to your feed, so that they can keep up with your posts every day from right within their favorite feed reader, without ever having to visit your blog every day just to see if there's anything new. If they found something new, then they could click over to your blog to read the full post.

This way, it's a win-win for both you and the subscriber.

It's a win for you because once you have a subscriber, you know that they are at least going to take a look at your headlines at some point – even if not daily, hopefully weekly. Feed subscription is a big plus also because now you don't have to deal with email formatting, testing, delivery, bounce rates, spam complaints, and email subscription management. Just post to your blog, and *fuhgedabouddit* – literally!

It's a win for your subscriber because you cannot force-feed them your feed – meaning, you cannot spam them with your feed (at least until the persistent spammers find a way to do even that).

RSS feeds are the purest, most glorious example of *permission marketing* (a word coined by Seth Godin at `sethgodin.typepad.com`). They can add you to their list of frequently read feeds, or they can delete you whenever they want. They decide if they get to see you. No more trying to unsubscribe and reaching a dead link, or a message that says you will be unsubscribed "shortly" (and you still keep getting emails anyway). No more opt-out hell for your subscribers – feeds are like opt-out-on-steroids.

Leveraging Social Networks

Digg, Reddit and Furl

Tightly-woven communities like Digg.com, Reddit.com. Furl.net and Del.icio.us can send you a large amount of traffic practically overnight.

These are large communities with (mostly) like-minded individuals with more or less the same kind of demographics – meaning, similar interests, tastes, skills and even age - with a huge amount of traffic coming in to the main site. Any news item or link that makes it to the home page or category home page of these sites can result in an instantaneous surge in traffic – to such an extent that sites have been known to completely shut down operations temporarily, unable to handle the increase in load as a result of the sudden inflow of new visitors.

I have witnessed web sites replacing their database-driven, image- and text- heavy home pages with a light-weight, text-only, static web page carrying an announcement that practically blames these sites for crashing their servers, and asking me to come back and try again later.

What's the point in creating a web site and doing a thousand different things to drive traffic to your site, if as soon as you get that traffic, you have to take your site down?

This is one of the reasons why you need to have professional hosting (even if shared) from say a Hostrocket.biz or Dream-host.biz (hosts I use myself), but the main point here is that these sites can send you so many visitors, that it can literally bring your server to its knees. That's how powerful these communities are.

Of course, anything that is powerful and has great potential will end up getting into both the right hands and the wrong hands. In the recent past, many spammy-services have sprung up which promise you a "Home page entry" on sites like Digg, in return for money, of course. Then they use their army of spammers who use a variety of user names and locations and IP addresses to artificially try and boost the ranking of the site being promoted, and try to get to the home page, which really is the jackpot for site owners.

Like in real life, as spammers come up with more ideas to abuse the system, the system (the software and the community) tries to adapt itself to beat the spammers. So, these communities are continuously evolving to maintain the integrity of their systems.

But, as a legitimate content developer, you can use these communities to your advantage to drive a lot of traffic to your blogs and web sites.

Also, every site submitted to these sites results in a number of legitimate back-links to your site – and because these sites are considered "authority sites" by search engines due to their credibility, traffic and content, any incoming links from these sites goes a long way towards improving your PageRank. So, even if your site doesn't make it to the home page, just the back-links alone make it worth developing great content and submitting the post's URL to these sites.

Especially when you have a new blog or web site, you should post every new blog-post or article to not just one or two, but to all of the social networks, which can get your site out of the sandbox sooner than later.

You can use services like `AddThis.com` or `FeedButton.com` which provide you with ready-made images and HTML code that makes it simple for your users to add your content to these networks.

In fact, right after you "publish" each post or article, you could yourself add your content to each and every one of these social networks proactively, rather than waiting for someone to just stumble upon your content and add your content on their own.

Yes, some would call this sneaky – but I call it proactive-promotion. This is the exact same strategy as building a web site and submitting it to the various search engines and directories - nothing illegal or illegitimate about it.

And there's no faster way to get your web site ranked and boost your PageRank than to blog-and-ping these social networks, like we saw earlier, as well as blog-and-bookmark.

Tools For Promoting Your Feed

Feeds are similar to web pages. You can track the number of subscribers, the number of posts viewed, the number of times your feed is downloaded versus how many actual clicked through to your blog, which posts were clicked on, what feed readers are your subscribing, and so on.

There are a number of commercial tools available for this, the most popular one being FeedBurner.com. I use this for my own blogs to track usage and subscription.

Monetizing Your Feed

This is the trickiest part of the RSS-feed-subscription strategy.

One thing you have to know right at the beginning, before you even get into blogging, is that blogging has many different advantages – both monetary and non-monetary.

To earn direct revenue from your blog, it will take a lot of effort in building high-quality content and driving lots of traffic to your blog.

There are three ways in which you can directly monetize your blog:

- Pay-Per-Click (PPC) advertising
- Cost-Per-Action (CPA) advertising (affiliate programs)

- Cost-Per-iMpression (CPM) advertising (branding)
- Selling your own products

Pay-Per-Click Advertising (for Blogs)

This is arguably the *least* profitable, depending on your target audience. Blogs – and sites - that are oriented towards the moms-and-pops – the average, not very tech-savvy audience – can earn well with PPC ads. But it's a catch-22 because the very fact that your audience is visiting a "blog" means that they are reasonably tech-savvy.

If they even know what a blog is, and what a feed-reader is, and have subscribed to your blog, then they are already in the "won't-click-on-ads" group.

The more internet-savvy and computer-savvy people are, the less they tend to click on ads. If you are reading this book, you are obviously pretty 'net-savvy yourself. So, think about it: when was the last time you clicked on a PPC ad on a blog that you visit regularly? Forget PPC ads – when was the last time you clicked on any ad – be it PPC, banners, or buried-in-content affiliate links?

Most of the traffic from social networks like Digg.com and Reddit.com will be mostly geeks and nerds. Now I'm an avid blogger, digger, googler, you know - the self-proclaimed "uber-web savvy" type. And I won't be too far off the mark when I say that the tech profile of the average digg user will be quite similar to mine - and I can't remember the last time I clicked on an Adsense ad.

I have many friends and family members (wife, B.I.L) who are in IT, and almost none of them ever click on Google Adsense ads, not even on Google's own search pages, let alone on 3rd-party web sites. When they do a Google search, they are completely and utterly focused on the organic search results, and completely block out the ad-block on the right-side of the page. This is not a Digg- or Reddit- specific phenomenon. I think this is more of a natural, human phenomenon.

I'm one of Google's biggest proponents. I sign up for most Google services the day they are beta-launched. But my Google-fanboi status notwithstanding, I am predicting that Adsense's effectiveness is only going to decline, the way CTR's for banners decreased.

Here's why: Google's text ads were novel for a while, and everyone clicked on them, similar to the novelty of banners and popups when they were first introduced. They're now common place, and I have increasingly noticed through my various web sites that the average non-techie visitors are among the few left clicking on them, and the tech-savvy folks are *ignoring* them at an alarmingly increasing rate.

I say that with substantial proof, because on my web sites built for the average mom and pop, the Adsense CTR's are very high - and my earnings substantial. But on my sites targeted towards a tech-savvy audience, the CTR's are pathetic, and revenue is nothing to write home about.

This is why you see popular tech blogs and sites going with pay-for-placement or pay-per-impression ads.

Here's a real-world example: Imagine blogging for a whole year, ending up with a very popular blog that has 23,457 subscribers, ranked #45 out of all blogs in the world, and earning (brace yourself) a whopping $3,350 for the entire year! Now stop imagining - this stuff is real. I'm talking about Guy Kawasaki's blog (`blog.guykawasaki.com`). These statistics only goes to prove my theory further, that:

It is very hard to get tech-savvy folks to click on ads the way the average surfers (moms-and-pops) do.

It is not easy making a living just by blogging.

I myself own a site targeted at moms-and-pops, and I made many, many times more than what Guy's #45-ranked blog earned. And mine is a very small niche, and a lot, lot, *lot* less less popular than Guy's blog.

Here are some key stats from his blog:

- 2,436,117 page views (about 6,200/day)
- 23,457 RSS feed subscribers
- Total advertising revenue: **$3,350 for 1 entire year** (= $1.39 cpm)

You've got to take these stats with a pinch of salt, because these stats could be skewed due to a number of things – especially due to improper optimization for Adsense (or ads in general). Like mentioned earlier, Adsense optimization requires a lot of continued experimentation and tracking – in other words, a lot of focused effort - in order to make it work, which I'm guessing Guy probably didn't due for various reasons.

However, this is not very different from the occasional, low CPMs (Cost Per-thousand iMpressions) that I've seen often with my own Adsense, even on my for-moms-and-pops sites.

This drop was usually not because of number of click-thru's or the click-thru rate (both of which have actually gone up due to my persistent optimization of the content and the ad placements), but actually due to a big fall in the CPM.

As the number of advertisers on any given day increases or decreases, so too will your earnings-per-click; more competition means more earnings-per-click, and less competition means less earnings-per-click.

Decrease in CPM could be because advertisers are generally bidding lower, or the advertisers in a specific niche are bidding lower, or that Google somehow (read smart-pricing) has determined that your click-throughs are worth less than before due to poor conversion rates, or it could simply mean that Google is taking a bigger chunk of the earnings-per-click. It could be one, or more, or all – there's no real way to tell.

That is why Adsense earnings cannot be treated as a *static* statistic – it could vary day-to-day.

The key to monetizing your blog or web site with advertisement revenue is to *experiment* – with colors, positioning, keywords, content and even alternate ad providers other than Adsense. Google is not the be-all, end-all, even though I've found it to be certainly the most profitable, and *consistently* profitable at that.

It may not necessarily work the same for you – maybe you will make more with other ad services than Adsense, or not. You will never know unless you experiment, and track, and adapt.

The bottom-line is that I believe PPC will gradually make way for PPP (pay-per-performance - like affiliate programs) ads - and it is known that Google is developing a CPA (Cost Per Action) service for this. And then they will compete with the LinkShares and CommissionJunctions of the world.

As long as they keep evolving Adsense, Google will be fine, but the quality of clicks on PPC is only going to deteriorate, as more people find out that every click = someone makes money + someone loses money.

Cost-Per-Action Advertising

Similar to PPC, these types of ads also may not work on a tech-savvy audience. But if you promote the right kind of products that are closely related to your content, especially with inline-ads (where you weave the ads right into your content), then you have a much better chance of making money with your blog than using just plain PPC.

Cost-Per-Impression (Branding) Advertising

Currently, this is probably among the top revenue earning strategy for bloggers. The more traffic your blog has, the more advertisers will pay to place branding ads (banners, video, links, and images) on your blog.

You could potentially make thousands of dollars from CPM ads if you are able to attract a large number of visitors. In fact this is exactly how Yahoo and MSN and other big sites monetize their millions of web pages and communities.

Of course, you won't get the same rates as the big guys, but you don't need to make millions like they do, as you have 0 employees, or maybe a handful at most – and every single penny you earn is a profit, because your blog costs you just $10 ($50 tops, if you subscribe to paid services like Feedburner.com) a month to maintain!

Selling Your Own Products

If you get a large amount of traffic to your blog, these are obviously interested in what you have to offer, and may also be interested in products that you have created. So, instead of advertising other people's products, you could promote your own products and services, and sell more of your own stuff to your audience. That way, you get the biggest chunk of the deal, and not worry about making pennies on the dollars from other advertisers. You are the advertiser here, and you get to keep the biggest piece of the profits.

Look at the blogs of Seth Godin and Guy Kawasaki – they don't really sell any real products – they themselves are the product that they are promoting. Their blogs promote their brand and their expertise – which results in higher sales of their books, and more customers for their business presentations and seminars.

In fact, if you can deliver quality content through your blog frequently and consistently, you can build up such a loyal subscriber base, that you could sell thousands of copies of your book the day your book goes on sale – and maybe even before it goes on sale!

Which is the best strategy?

Ultimately, you need to approach it like your investments – do not put all your eggs in one basket, and have a diversified portfolio, and don't be afraid to pull the plug on bad investments.

Try multiple ad providers, experiment with headlines, content, placements, PPC, CPA, affiliate programs – use a healthy mix of all types of ad channels, and most importantly, don't forget to make notes and keep track of everything you do.

19. Ravi Recommends

I have created a *super-list* with both free and not-free products that you will need to run your ebusiness.

Remember, that the more free stuff you try to get-by with, the longer it will take for you to get going and start making some money, because there is always a price to pay, even when something is free. When it is free, the price isn't be money, but probably the extra time spent, the extra effort you have to put in, or the extra complexity that it brings with it..

Products are listed in order of decreasing importance. So, **Email**: Eudora, Thunderbird means that I recommend Eudora the first, and for some reason if you can't use or don't wish to use *Eudora,* only then consider the second choice *Thunderbird*. Also note that I may have specified the Not-Free version first, but in some cases the free version may be listed first – which means it is either better than the best non-free version (believe it or not, that does happen!), or that the free version gives you almost everything you need to get your work done, and that the frills and specials in the non-free version may not be really required.

Legend

F: Free, **NF**: Not Free

HTML editor
Dreamweaver (NF): `Adobe.com/products/dreamweaver/`
NVu (F): `Nvu.com`

FTP client
FileZilla (F): `Filezilla.sourceforge.net`
CuteFTP (NF): `CuteFTP.com`

Text editor
Notepad++ (F) : `Notepadplusplus.sourceforge.net`
TextPad (F): `Textpad.com`

Image Editor
Gimp (F): `Gimp.org`
Photoshop (NF): `Adobe.com/products/photoshop`

Stock Photos
`iStockPhoto.com` (NF): For inexpensive photos to use in your content
`wiki.creativecommons.org/Image` : More free/non-free photo sites

Documents and Presentation
`OpenOffice.org` (F): Full office suite
Microsoft Office (NF): Full office suite
Google Docs (F): `docs.google.com` – Web-based docs and spreadsheets

Email
Eudora (F): `Eudora.com`
Thunderbird (F): `Mozilla.com/en-US/thunderbird/`

Blog
`WordPress.org` (F): installed blog software
`WordPress.com` (F): hosted, online blog service
`Blogger.com` (F): hosted, online blog service
`TypePad.com` (NF): hosted, online blog service

Community
Joomla CMS (F): `Joomla.org`
Drupal CMS (F): `Drupal.org`
phpBB forums (F): `phpBB.com`

No Business Like E-Business – NBLEB.com

Autoresponder

AutoresponsePlus.com (NF): installed software
AWeber.com (NF): Hosted online service
1SiteAutomation.com (NF): Hosted online service

Web Hosting

Hostrocket.biz
Dream-Host.biz
iPower-Web.com

Affiliate Programs and PPC/CPA services

Google.com/Adsense (includes Google Referrals)
CJ.com
LinkShare.com
ClickBank.com
Amazon.com
Text-Link-Ads.com
Bidvertiser.com

Google Tools To Keep An Eye On

Adsense: Google.com/adsense
Adwords: Google.com/adwords
Sitemaps: Google.com/webmasters/sitemaps/
Analytics: Google.com/analytics
Checkout: Google.com/checkout
Apps for your domains: Google.com/a
Google Reader: Google.com/reader
Gmail: Gmail.com
Notebook: Google.com/notebook
Calendar: Google.com/calendar
Maps: Google.com/maps
Blog search: Google.com/blogsearch

Other Cool Sites and Web Apps

Notepad.yahoo.com
LinkOverLoad.com
FeedBurner.com (NF)
AddThis.com

Video Hosting
YouTube.com
Video.Aol.com
Veoh.com

Social Networks & Communities
Technorati.com
Digg.com
Reddit.com
Netscape.com
StumbleUpon.com
Del.icio.us

Multimedia
Audacity.sourceforge.net : Free audio editor that can record and play audio, import and export different audio file formats, edit your sound tracks, mix tracks, and apply effects.

Camstudio.org: Software that can record all screen and audio activity on your computer and create industry-standard AVI video files and using its built-in SWF Producer can turn those AVIs into lean, mean, bandwidth-friendly Streaming Flash videos (SWFs)

DVDflick.net: It can take video files stored on your computer and turn them into a DVD that will play back on your DVD player or media center. You can add additional custom audio tracks as well as subtitles.

RSS Feeds
* FeedBurner.com: To track usage of your feeds; provides extensive stats.
* AddMe.com, FeedButton.com, Ekstreme.com/socializer: All three services give your users a unified, easy-to-use bookmark and feed subscription interface. I use AddMe on my blog, and Socializer for the blog-and-bookmark strategy.
* Magpierss.sourceforge.net: PHP script for reading and displaying RSS feeds on your web site.

For more recommendations, visit RaviRecommends.com

20. Registering a Domain Name

The first thing you need for your web site is a domain name – like www.Example.com - which is nothing but a unique name for your web site – just like your phone number or your email address. This is what people use to look you up on the Internet. This is the address of your online store – where you can sell physical products, downloadable digital products, or your services.

Business Name and Domain Name

It always confuses me when I hear an ad on the radio for a product that I want to buy, and they end the ad with an 800 (toll free) number. To make matters worse, there are 888, 877, 866 and other toll-free area codes - which make it practically impossible for me to remember the number, unless I heard the ad repetitively many times over (which in reality is actually the core strategy behind radio advertising – to advertise over and over again until the message is etched in the mind of the listener) and even then, with someone like me with short-term memory issues, the ad doesn't stand much of a chance.

Instead, they could simply include their web site domain name at the end of the ad along with the phone number. But in spite of the very obvious reasons as to why you should do it, not all companies do. Make sure you are not among them.

Yes, there used to be a time when most people did not have access to a computer, leave alone the Internet. But today, almost everyone has access to the web – most at work or home, and others at the local public library.

Try to register at least one domain name that is the same as your business name. If your haven't started your business yet, you may want to first find out what domain names are available, register it immediately, and then name your business based on that name.

Of course, when it comes to direct marketing, a domain name really isn't all that important. You can popularize any domain name you want using Pay-Per-Click advertising and affiliate marketing. But it still doesn't hurt to have your domain name the same as your business name, mainly for brand consistency.

Your brand name needs to be consistent, whether it is your business name, your domain name, the name that comes up on your customer's credit card statement, your DBA ("Doing Business As") name, or even the email addresses that you use to contact your visitors, newsletter subscribers, business contacts or customers.

Using it in Your Email Address

Why would you want to use an unprofessional looking Joe1965@hotmail.com or vz19865@verizon.com when you can have Joe@JoeSomebody.com ?

Free web-mail accounts are for personal use. Don't even *think* about using them for your business.

How would you feel about purchasing a product by credit card from a web site which lists only a P.O Box address and a Yahoo.com email address? Would you be comfortable giving out your credit card information to someone who can't even get a proper domain name email address or a proper business address?

Why You Need a Good Domain Name

Your web site is your home online. You need a good name – that is easy to remember, easy to pronounce, easy to spell, and short enough to type (we will also deal with long domain names later, but in a different context).

A good domain name shouldn't have hyphens (dashes). Imagine a long domain name like...

`Theres-No-Business-Like-Ebusiness.com`

...with multiple dashes in it, and spelling it over the phone to a prospective customer or business associate.

Preferably try to get something that ends with a .com rather than .net or .org. The extension .COM is commonly used for commercial web sites. .net is its less popular cousin, and .org is generally used by organizations, mostly not-for-profit ones.

True, there are many `.net` and `.org` web sites that make more money than most `.com`'s. But that's not the point. Those are the exceptions to the rule.

When I thought of the name Webmaster In A Box, I discovered that `WebmasterInABox.com` was already taken. So, I had no choice but to register WebmasterInABox.net. I wasn't too happy about it, but I preferred doing this than registering a plain domain name for which the .com version was available.

When I verbally gave out my web site name during a conversation, most of my friends and family could easily remember the first part – "WebmasterInABox" – because it was kind of unusual and catchy – but they all ended up typing "WebmasterInABox*.com*" by habit – and complained to me later that they couldn't get to my web site (of course, whoever registered the .com version, never put up an actual site at that Internet address).

Get a domain name that matches your company's name or leading product's name. People usually end up associating your web site with your product or company name – which is the domain name they will look for when trying to visit your web site. And if your domain name is something completely unrelated, they may never find you – worse still is that they may find your site, but may think it's the wrong site because what they see looks or sounds nothing like what they heard about.

Alternatively, since good domain names are hard to come by (all 2, 3, 4 and probably 5 lettered English words have already been registered as .com's, .net's or .org's.). But there is hope. There are more TLDs (Top Level Domains – the part of the domain name after the last "." [dot]) available now – like .biz, .tv, .us, .name amd .info.

Cyber-Squatting

You cannot register names that belong to celebrities, trademarks, or even well-established companies, brand or product names.

Don't even think of `MicrosoftConsulting`.com, `GoogleAdAgency`.net, `AppleHardwareStore`.biz. Nope, not even Madonna.com or ParisHilton.com.

Whether or not your business is related to these big trademarks and company and individual names, you can still get into trouble if you tried to infringe on them.

If you are a very small local business in an unrelated area of business (Microsoft Pest Control, say), it is possible that you might get away with the name for a period of time – when you are probably not worth the time of these large corporations.

If you start having a negative impact on the brand name, or if they start getting unwanted publicity because of your company, or if your products have anything related to their line of business or if you are a potential competitor, then their legal teams are going to come after you even before you can think of an alternative name.

Classic example: "Lindows.com". This Linux flavored operating system maker, coined the name probably combining LINux and winDOWS. For the first few years, Microsoft didn't bother. Eventually, as the product started gaining market share and started getting popular, they went after Lindows, and forced the name change to "Linspire".

Why bother with the expensive legal hassle of taking on these big companies or celebrities with deep pockets? You are better of creating your own identity and brand right from the start – and not have to bother about name changes midstream, which could affect your brand name, popularity and ultimately the bottom-line.

What's in a Name?

In the good ol' dot-bomb days, a very big deal was made out of domain names. `Business.com` was sold for $7.5 Million and `Loans.com` fetched about $3 Million.

Are domain names really worth that much? Not any more. History has proven to us that a name by itself isn't worth anything.

Think about it – when you want to buy books, would you go to `Books.com` or `Amazon.com`? When you want to research car models and dealer pricing, would you go to `Cars.com` or `Edmunds.com`? If you wanted to buy branded sneakers, would you go to a generic, brand-less `Shoes.com` or that of a popular brand like `Nike.com` or `Adidas.com`?

Do you think `Amazon.com` would've been any more successful if it had the name `Books.com`? I don't think so.

A name is only as good as the product behind it, the people behind it and most importantly, the marketing behind it.

Be Creative

So what if all regular words are already taken? Why not be creative and make up your own name?

Take a hint - three of the biggest e-businesses online have off-beat domain names that have nothing to do with their actual business - `Google.com` (from the mathematical term "Googol"), `Yahoo.com`, `Amazon.com` (totally unrelated to books or consumer products).

Other similar domain names include `Edmunds.com` (nothing to do with cars), `Monster.com` (unrelated to recruiting), and `Apple.com` (unrelated to fruits).

What I Use

I use `Godaddy.com` for their amazing centralized domain management control panel, awesome phone and email support, and most importantly, very inexpensive yearly registration fees.

You also get a *Transfer Concierge,* a service where a live person is available to help you transfer your domain names from high-fees registrars some of whom charge thrice the price that you pay at `Godaddy.com`.

Note of warning: I have heard from a couple of heavy-hitting Internet marketers that when they do major product launches, their super affiliates (big-name partners) tend to send out thousands of emails. Due to these large number of emails getting sent around pretty much around the same time (just days before the launch), if one of the recipients of those emails happens to make a spam complaint about the email, regardless of the validity of the complaint, it is said that Godaddy has been known to literally take over and suspend the domain name (specified in the email, assuming it has also been registered at Godaddy), which means all visitors trying to reach that domain name will see some kind of a warning message from Godaddy instead of seeing the actual web site.

When you are in the midst of a big launch generating tens of thousands of leads, the last thing you want those potential buyers to see is that you are being accused of spam and that your domain name has been suspended (possibly pending enquiry, but still!).

Now, I do not have any direct proof that Godaddy indeed did this, and neither do I know for a fact that none of the super affiliates sent out any spam.

Personally, I have never had any issues with Godaddy, and I still recommend them highly, and they are also my primary registrar with whom I have almost 90% of my domain names registered.

So, I leave it to you to decide. Anyway, the backup registrar I use is NameCheap.com, who is apparently "ask first, shoot later" versus other registrar's "shoot first, ask later".

21. Web Hosting

This is a service provider who provides you with hard disk space to store all the files that make up your web site, in a central location online where anyone, anywhere in the world with Internet access can access them simply by typing your domain name – www.Example.com - in their web browser.

This is the space you rent or own (we'll get to the difference shortly) – only it is online – where you display your products and merchandise.

Virtual Hosting

This is where your web site is located on the same computer as 20-30 other web sites, belonging to different businesses or individuals. Consider this similar to renting space in a mall – where your neighbors are other stores, many related to your line of business.

The advantage is, that it costs less, because you are renting. When it comes to web hosting, renting is cheaper than owning (unlike in the world of real estate where owning is better than renting).

That is because you do not have the expertise to take care of all the stuff that goes into hosting a web site – nor can the average person afford to hire a team of techies for thousands of dollars a year in salaries just for this, when you can get virtual hosting for as little as $3 per month.

Basically, think of it as "outsourcing" your web hosting needs. You do not want the headaches of web hosting, period.

When you are starting out, it makes more sense to get virtual hosting.

Dedicated Hosting

When you sign up for dedicated hosting, you get your own server, with your site being the only site hosted on this server. The hosting company (host) owns this server which is located in their data center along with the other servers. The host also provides you all the basic networking and hardware support, and the infrastructure for you to remotely log in to your server and install your own software and services.

You also have the option of having your server fully managed, in which case you are assigned a tech support representative, who will take care of your software needs too. Obviously, if you manage the server yourself, it is going to be less expensive than having your host support you, which comes at a price because they have to have personnel assigned to you.

Dedicated hosting can be a great option for someone who has outgrown virtual hosting, and needs more control over their server, not to mention the need to not share the server with other web site owners, because the more sites with different owners hosted on the server, the more vulnerable it is not only to security attacks (because not everyone may adhere to the same security standards as you site), but also to the server availability (because some webmaster somewhere ran a script which crashed your server and the server had to be restarted, which affects all web sites located on that server).

Co-Location

This is where you purchase your own server, you have your own server admin, but the hosting company just physically locates it in their datacenter and provides you with networking and basic hardware support, giving you access to remotely log-in to the server to maintain it yourself, while also giving you the ability to reboot your server remotely.

This works for medium to large businesses that have their own IT personnel, and only need to outsource their datacenter needs like networking, backups and bandwidth.

When you are starting out, look no further than virtual hosting, as it will allow you to get started for only a couple of dollars a month, and give you everything you need to run a web site, until you get large enough and your site gets popular enough, where you need to upgrade to dedicated hosting.

What to Look for in a Web Host

There are certain features to keep in mind when selecting a web host. Here is a list, in no particular order:

Linux Hosting

Make sure they are Linux-based (Linux is one of the most popular flavors of UNIX). Windows is great for your desktop, but when it comes to web hosting, you simply cannot beat Linux (or other flavor of Unix). Also, more open source third-party products are available – and are also better suited - for Linux, which will add up to tremendous cost savings as your web site grows.

Bandwidth Quota

A typical web page on a web site is typically made up of a number of files: a HTML page that shows things in different colors, bold text, etc; a CSS file that keeps styles consistent across pages; images and banners; JavaScript files, and so on.

Every time you access a web page online, all such files that make up the page you are trying to access, are first downloaded to your hard disk (to a temporary directory – like *c:\windows\temp*) and then it is assembled by your web browser (Internet explorer or FireFox) and then displayed on your screen.

So, if you access a page that is made up of a 50 KB page, has 40 KB of images, and a 10 KB JavaScript file, then the total is 100 KB. So, every time you access this page, it costs the site owner 100KB of bandwidth – so 100 KB is subtracted from his total monthly quota – almost like cell phone minutes usage.

So, if the site owner has 10 GB of available bandwidth, then if his home page is accessed 100,000 times, his monthly quota will be exhausted.

Obviously, a web site has many web pages, each about 50KB – 100KB in size (average). So, each visitor may view many pages during one visit – which means, all that bandwidth can add up pretty fast.

So, make sure you have a reasonable amount of bandwidth available to you each month. When you are starting out, having around 10GB is a good start.

Bandwidth Options and Overage Charges

As your web site grows, your web site traffic is also going to grow exponentially. So, make sure your web host offers you good upgrade packages without costing too much extra. Also, check the price of each additional GB of bandwidth, if you happen to go over your allotted limit in a month.

Scripting Options

Make sure you can run PHP and Perl scripts on your site. Almost all small e-Business web programming is written in either Perl or PHP. You can do almost nothing with your web site if you cannot run scripts. Plus most open source software – which is also free - have been developed in PHP and Perl which will go a long way in stretching your limited budget.

Also, PHP is a very easy, fun language to learn, and learning PHP is something to consider for the long term - you can soon be programming like a pro if you have the aptitude.

MySQL Database

If you want to do anything interesting with your web site, you need to be able to hook it up to a database. Storing information in a database makes it very easy to update and retrieve.

This information could be your product catalog, complete with product ID, description, thumbnails and larger pictures, pricing information, special discounts, bonuses, etc.

Or it could be membership information for your customers, affiliates, partners, vendors, newsletter subscribers, etc.

Make sure your web hosting account comes with a MySQL database. MySQL is a free, open-source database that almost all web hosts provide as part of their packages.

Other Features to Watch Out For

At least a 30-day money back guarantee so that you can try out the service and support before you get locked in to a package.

Unlimited pop email accounts, email forwarders and auto responders (out-of-office type emails)

Responsive phone, online and email support

Large pre-installed script library for both Perl and PHP: Very useful if you want to run image processing applications, like an online album, or other community-building.

Online Control Panel so that you can manage your entire web site using just a browser.

Multiple FTP accounts

Ability to set up Cron Jobs (automated tasks that can run scripts or carry out other repetitive tasks).

Ability to add-on SSL (to serve secure pages): You won't need this right away, but the upgrade should at least be possible.

Great Customer Service and Technical Support

Since you don't have physical access to the computer on which it is hosted, it is very important to have 24x7 technical support and friendly customer service.

What I Use

The web hosts I use myself, and highly recommend are HostRocket.biz and Dream-host.biz.

22. Web Site Design – The Norm

You will need more than just this book to learn about how to design simple yet visually pleasing and most importantly "usable" and powerful web sites that can sell.

Design is more than just how pretty-looking your web site is, how awesome your logo is, how fast loading your graphics are, or how cool your Flash animation is. Design is all about making your visitor take the *action* you want them to.

The *target action* could be one or more of the following - signing up for your newsletter, making a purchase, recommending your site to others, or even just browse through your site and click on Adsense ads.

Design is what helps remove all possible obstacles from your visitor's path, and drive them towards this *target action*.

Design is not just looks, but it also involves abstract concepts – like how your visitor "feels" while browsing through your web site - how trustworthy your web appears, how comfortable it makes her feel, and how trustworthy it is to make her give you her credit card information.

Some of the more tangible concepts of design are: Easy to use navigation links to help your visitor find what they want easily and quickly on your site, fast loading pages, the right information at the right place (like contact information), look and feel that says that you are a professional who has a legitimate product - and are not a fly-by-night operator.

Your web site should be intuitive – it shouldn't require a site map to help the visitor find his way through. The design and the content should gently lead the visitor sub-consciously to the ultimate goal – clicking on the "Buy Now" button.

Your web site should have a logical structure where the sections are well defined to improve usability, yet seamless enough to not make it seem like they are different web sites forcibly glued together.

It is hard enough to make a sale even after your visitor has added your product to the shopping cart and has already pulled out his wallet. Don't make it harder by posing obstacles to the sale – like asking for information at the wrong point in the sale; or asking for too much or too little; or confusing the visitor with insufficient or contradicting information; or distracting your visitor from the ultimate goal of making the purchase, by surrounding the sale pages with unnecessary information or links, to unrelated or unwanted parts of your web site or other third-party web sites.

Look and Feel (L&F)

Logos

Do not give too much importance to logos, unless you are a large corporation with branding consultants who you pay thousands of dollars a year just to tell you that the color scheme of your logo will make a difference to your bottom-line.

If you must have a logo, then at least make sure it is professionally designed – and is consistent with your company's brand.

If you don't know what a "brand" is, or don't have one yet, then don't sweat it - you can still make money online without knowing what it means.

However, when you are just starting out, this is a completely unnecessary expense. I would say don't worry about having a logo till you have started making some sales.

After 4 years online making thousands of dollars in sales every single month, WebmasterInABox.net still doesn't have a logo.

Images

Images can help with the visual impact of your product – and the content of your web site and copy – provided you get it right.

Don't use images unless you have to. Obviously, if you are selling physical goods, you have to make sure your product images are high quality and high resolution. Display only thumb-nails (smaller images) of your products on your sales pages, and display clearly the link that your visitor can click to view a larger version of the same image.

Make sure you also link the thumbnail image itself to the larger image, as people commonly try to move their mouse-over images to see if they lead them elsewhere.

Make sure this larger image has much more detail, is of quite high resolution and has excellent picture quality.

If your product is small in actual size (or large, for that matter), display it in the context of another image – like a hand, or a palm, or a finger – or the picture of a person standing in front of it or next to it – to give your visitor a better sense of how small (or large) it truly is.

HTML: Your First Four-Lettered Word

HTML stands for Hyper Text Markup Language. It is the most basic and most popular language for creating web sites.

HTML is what makes words appear **bold**, *italicized*, large and small, tabular and linear, bulleted and tabbed etc, and adds basic look and feel to a web site.

If you are a beginner and wanted to learn just one language to help you out in managing your web sites, then this is the one I suggest. However, there are design tools available that mostly eliminate the need to know HTML and JavaScript (see next section).

These HTML editors are also known as WYSIWIG (What You See Is What You Get) tools. Such an editor will let you create and edit web pages, while also allowing you to visually see what the final result looks like as you are designing your pages.

You don't need to get too technical and start learning HTML and JavaScript right away. But in the long run, it will help you get things done quicker and better, if you know a little bit of what goes under the hood of these web pages.

Not just that, HTML editors are extremely useful in saving you lots of typing time, designing and formatting time, and lots of painstaking effort in getting the look "just right".

DreamWeaver vs. FrontPage

The only HTML editor I recommend is Macromedia's DreamWeaver (`Adobe.com/products/dreamweaver`)

I highly recommend that you **do not** use Microsoft's FrontPage. FrontPage, as with most Microsoft products, has a way of adding Microsoft's proprietary gobble-de-gook to your pages, which will not only prevent you from hosting your web site on Unix-based web hosts (which are much cheaper than Windows-based web hosts), but will also make your code "non-standard" which means industry standard tools and software will not work well with it. And this means you will be forced to choose Microsoft's products at many junctions of web site development.

Furthermore, you will end up hosting only on web hosts that support FrontPage, which will in the long run mean more expenses to you when you start expanding your site to include dynamic programming.

Also, Microsoft-based products are more lenient in letting you get away with non-standard practices (like not being case sensitive, or using spaces in file names and directory names), using FrontPage extensions etc, that soon your site will become so non-standard, it will not be compatible with anything non-Microsoft.

DreamWeaver is the only real option – and that is what you should be using. It does cost a couple of hundred dollars – but what you pay up-front will save you thousands of times over in terms of time and effort saved. Not just that - DreamWeaver will help you do stuff that most editors can only fantasize about. So, go on and download a trial version of DreamWeaver from Adobe.com, and you'll know why I'm such a big fan.

Using JavaScript

JavaScript is another elementary programming language that adds some interactivity to static, dull web sites that are made up of just plain HTML.

Like warning you with alerts when you miss out filling a form field, ability to open windows of precise size, hiding and showing paragraphs of text to increase readability, usage of cookies to store your preferences and make it a better experience, and so on, JavaScript is used wherever you need to make a page a little more interactive, and to save unnecessary trips back to your server (thus saving web server resources).

Designing with CSS

HTML pages are usually arranged into sections - the top header, the left navigation bar, the main body area, the right tools and miscellaneous content section, and finally the footer.

If you designed these with HTML Tables, then if you decided to later switch the navigation to the right and the tools section to the left, then it is much harder to do so without physically changing the content of the page – and this becomes even more tedious if you have to do this to multiple (as your site grows, to hundreds of) pages.

CSS – Cascading Style Sheets – are a better option for setting site wide preferences in terms of look and feel.

Using one single file you can control the site wide font style, size, what various elements look like, where the various page elements (like header, body, navigation and footer) are displayed.

If at any point you want to make a site wide change, all you have to do is change just one single file, and all the pages on your web site – whether it is one page, or thousands of pages – will automatically reflect the changes when your visitor visits those pages.

Once again, don't worry about learning CSS for now. There are more important things to master first – like how to make money, for instance.

Site Navigation

Sitemaps

On many sites, you will see a link called "sitemap" which lists all of the links and categories and sections of the web site.

If your web site is logically and intuitively arranged, then your visitor won't, and shouldn't, need a site map. But recently, search engines like Google love sitemaps because they have links to all pages of your site, which in turn allows the spider to get to every corner of your web site.

If you have a lot of content, then start by dividing the content into various broad categories, like:

- About us
- Articles
- Help
- Products
- Services
- Contact Us
- Testimonials

If you sell only one product, you could even include a "Buy Now" link in your navigation menu.

You could then divide your categories further:

About us
- Who we are
- Our Vision

Contact Us

Press
- Press releases
- Press kit

Syndication
- Content reprint Information
- Content Syndication
- RSS Feeds

Articles

Partners
- Affiliates
- Resellers
- Vendors

You could also add what are called as "bread crumbs" at the top of the site – these are just links that show you how deep you are into the site., e.g., :

About us → Who we are → Our Vision

About us → Who we are → Meet the team

About us → Who we are → Contact Us

To Frame or Not To Frame?

Frames allow site designers to present web pages in the form of independent components that exist separately, each of them further divided into one or more sub-windows or sub-components.

To read the full technical explanation and to get a better idea, visit NBLEB.com/frames which will take you to the w3.org (World Wide Web Consortium's web site).

From a design perspective, I strongly recommend against using frames for commercial, sales-oriented web sites.

Frames are suited mostly for technical, tutorials-based web sites that have, say, a number of chapters and sub-chapters links to the left, in which case frames would provide better navigation between chapters for the reader. For almost all other sites, frames are simply a bad design option.

Frames primarily have a number of drawbacks.

Pages that use frames cannot be bookmarked

This is probably the most serious flaw. Of course, you can introduce some additional JavaScript programming to provide a work-around for this, but it only complicates the overall site navigation, and this is something you shouldn't even consider unless you really know what you are doing and are a pro at designing web sites.

Inconsistent across browsers

Different browsers display framed pages differently. It is rather difficult to make the pages look exactly the way you see them when you are designing them.

Printing issues

A visitor may not be able to correctly print out the section of the web page that she is interested in. In fact, the user may not even realize why all the printouts keep showing either just the navigation buttons, or the header banner on top, and may just leave your web site altogether because of frustration, rather than letting you know.

The only way you can make this fool-proof is by once again adding extra programming along with a "Print this" image and site design that involves a lot of programming and site architecture knowledge than you would want to know even in a life time.

No one has the time to deal with site-viewing issues. If your visitor can't figure it out in 5 seconds, she will be gone just as fast.

Programming Issues

It makes it very ugly for another site to deep-link to a page on your web site. In fact, many sites may wish to put a small horizontal frame around all external sites, so that their visitors can go back to the original site after they're done visiting you.

If you use frames yourself, then the programming on your site and the referring site may clash, and the end result could be in ugly JavaScript errors and prompts, and even the browser crashing in extreme cases.

So, just say no – to cigarettes, drugs and frames.

SSI and Page Templates

SSI (Server Side Includes) is a rather outdated technology. This is used to include dynamic programming into regular pages.

With the arrival of scripting language PHP, SSI becomes almost too complex to develop and set up. PHP accomplishes the same end-result, but is much more fun and easy to learn, and also gives you a tremendous amount of power in terms of making your web site dynamic.

So, if you are really keen on learning a programming language, let it be PHP (`PHP.net`) which is a fun, free, easy to learn and open source language. PHP has a very large community of users and developers, tons of free tutorials, help forums and online content available - that will offer you lots of support for learning PHP – all of it for free.

Using Ready-Made Site Templates

I highly recommend purchasing a ready-made template online sold by many web sites online – many of them available for free. These templates have a pre-built color scheme, graphics for the buttons, logo, screen layout, etc. Just add content and you have a web site ready to be published in less than 10 minutes.

A few sample templates have been included in the NBLEB Toolkit for you to use for free. You may use them commercially if you wish.

You will also need image editing software like Macromedia Fireworks, or Adobe PhotoShop if you wish to customize the logos and images to your web site's needs. To begin with, you could use the free image editor, GIMP (`gimp.org`).

Web Site Components

Here's a list of site components that you will need at the bare minimum.

Product Sales Page/Home Page

After your product, the next most important item is your sales page. This is the page which contains the sales pitch – in its simplest form, this could be just a picture of your product (if applicable) with lots of details about the benefits and features, persuasive marketing copy (text) that says why the visitor should buy the product, and why they should buy it from you rather than from a competitor (these "why's" are referred to as your "Unique Selling Proposition" or USP) and finally details about how to purchase the product.

Direct-Marketing Web Site

You have probably seen direct-marketing commercials on TV – especially those that come on later at night, selling all kinds of products from fitness equipment to weight-loss products to home, garden and kitchen items.

A direct marketing web site is one along those lines, commonly known in Internet Marketing lingo as a *mini-site.* This site has only about 1 to 3 pages, has direct-marketing styled copy – where you address the reader directly, and all statements are made in a casual conversational, informal tone, and made to sound like you, the site owner were talking directly to the visitor one-on-one. This kind of copy also moves at a relatively furious pace, and includes various powerful elements of direct marketing (as I will show you subsequently).

How to Write a Sales Page for a Mini-Site

The fastest way to learn about writing copy for a mini-site is by visiting the web sites of popular Internet marketers and trying to absorb from what they've done.

Here is a general overview of what is involved in a mini-site, with the elements in recommended order, top-to-bottom:

- The Heading
- Your product image
- The Sub-heading
- A powerful testimonial from someone well-known, if possible
- A high-energy introduction to your product
- Benefits of using your product (Note: I said benefits, not features)
- Features list – with each item stating the true benefit of that feature
- Call to action – This is where you ask for the purchase
- Your guarantee/warranty
- One or more **P.S.**'s (post script)
- Alternative action to take if end of page reached

However, not all web sites can be mini sites. Sometimes you need to have a little more elaborate web site. In such a case, you should consider adding the sections listed below, but only those appropriate for the product you are selling.

About Us

Your **About Us** page should be about who you (really) are – what your background is, why you started this web site, what your vision is for your product, what your credentials are. Avoid un-substantiated self-praise (*world's greatest software, the most powerful book ever sold*). However, if you can substantiate it, then this is definitely where you have to highlight it ("We are the #1 provider in the United States according to XYZ Marketers Consortium's 2006 Survey"), along with adding such powerful-but-true statements to your sales page too.

Contact Us

Clearly state all the ways in which your visitors and customers can contact you with pre- and post- sales questions, comments, concerns or suggestions.

Publish a contact-us form right on this page, and don't ask for too much information – the sender's name, email address, and their message should be sufficient for you to answer their email. Even make the subject optional if possible.

Clearly publish any telephone/pager/cell-phone number(s), timings during which they can contact you, how soon they can expect to hear from you, and what are the times during which you offer support or assistance.

Do not publish any "naked" email links (e.g. mailto: links) on this page, as they will get sucked up by spam bots (more on this in "Email Management", where I show you how to prevent spam).

Newsletter Signup Form

As you will read throughout this book, the money is in the list – I mean your *email* list. So, regardless of what other pages you have on your site, make sure one of the first things you create is a free newsletter that offers the reader weekly or bi-weekly tips, tricks or information on the same topic as your web site.

And you need to offer a quick sign up form on all pages of your site, preferably in the left top portion of the page, where it is clearly visible, possibly with some kind of incentive (free bonus – a ebook, some software, free info, etc) and ask them for at least their first name (so that you can personalize the emails) and their email address (of course).

F.A.Q

FAQ's can be a great place to provide answers to commonly asked questions, as well as questions you anticipate your visitors to have when they arrive at your web site.

Privacy Policy

It is very important to obviously let your potential newsletter subscribers know how you are going to use the information you collect about them – the more open you can be about this, the more signups you will get.

Testimonials

Documented proof about the quality of your product and your company from previous buyers and current clients will go a long way in establishing a sense of trust and confidence about your product.

Just make sure they are absolutely real, and provide as much information about the actual users as possible – without violating their privacy, of course (you could publish their web site name, which they would gladly welcome, as they get free publicity in return). Now, if you do mention the web site name, make sure it is not a "live link", meaning, it should not be clickable, as it can prove to be a distraction to your visitor and may distract him from purchasing your product if you send them away from your site to some other web site.

Remember, out of "site" is out of mind too.

As your web site starts to grow, here are some components that you should add, one at a time, without trying to add them all at the same time. See the next chapter "Web Site Programming" for a full list.

Develop Content

Probably the most powerful way to prove that you know what you are talking about, is by publishing a wide range of helpful content in which you share your expertise, experience, wisdom and offer tips, tricks and guidance and answer.

This might seem like an obvious thing to do, but if you pay attention to the various small e-Business web sites you visit, you will see that it really isn' obvious to too many (more about this in the chapter "Internet Marketing").

What I Use

Adobe DreamWeaver: For HTML editing.

Adobe Fireworks: For image editing.

Notepad++ (notepadplusplus.sourceforge.net) instead of Notepad: For quick text editing.

FileZilla (filezilla.sourceforge.net): For FTP'ing files to and from my web server.

DesktopDashboard.com text utilities for various other text utilities – say, like formatting my text newsletter to have only 65 characters per line (so that it doesn't word-wrap awkwardly when my newsletter subscribers view it in their browser or email client).

23. Email Management

You will be sending and receiving tons of emails managing and marketing your e-Business, so it is extremely important to be able to archive all emails sent and received, and also be able to sort and retrieve emails – like, say, all emails sent to a particular email address – sorted by date.

Also, you need to make sure that your software is well supported by the vendor, because you may need to store emails from many years. In fact, I have all emails sent and received from 1998 on my hard disk. Imagine how powerful all that information is when you realize I may have about a few hundred thousand contacts in there, who have emailed me over the years.

Email Client

Email storage and retrieval, is a major part of your e-Business, especially if you are a one-person show.

You need a consistent way to save and archive your emails over a period of time, and for this, you need an email "client" (desktop software that lets you download emails sent to you at your web site). This software also needs to have mature functionality and features to help you manage your emails – like the ability to search and retrieve messages quickly and efficiently.

Some of the common features you will need are:

- Ability to "pop" emails off of your web site's email storage (called POP servers) and be able to both leave a copy on your server, as well as delete all downloaded emails from your server (of course, after saving them on your computer first).
- Store emails on your hard disk for permanent storage
- Allow you to set up multiple email accounts for your various web sites, or even various email addresses on the same site
- Send outgoing emails from your different email addresses, based on which account you are using to send them
- Attach your signature(s) to all outgoing email (there is a better way to rotate signatures it with a Key-stroke Logger like VirtualTypingAssistant.com)
- Ability to filter incoming emails based on rules that you specify and sort them into various folders you have created – and even move messages to *trash* if required.

The only email client I recommend for is *Eudora* from Qualcomm (Eudora.com). An ad-supported free version – which is full-featured - is also available if you don't want to buy the commercial version.

I have used the ad-supported version for about 8 years now and I am absolutely crazy about Eudora, and I wouldn't know how to survive without it.

I strongly recommend against using Microsoft Outlook or Outlook Express as these products are more vulnerable to virus attacks. They have made vast improvements over the last several years to address this, but I have enough bad experiences with Microsoft products and viruses, that I still don't recommend them.

Managing Spam

You've heard the cliché "Prevention is better than cure". Nothing is truer than this statement, when it comes to spam.

In fact, spam is practically incurable. Once the bots (email collecting automated software ro**bots**) get to your email address, it is pretty much downhill from there – the most you can do is to detect them and remove them from your inbox, but you won't be able to make it completely go away.

The longer you display naked email addresses on your web site (naked meaning, displaying the plain email address in your web site copy as a mailto: link), more bots will suck up your email addresses, and the more spam you will get.

I am living proof for this – I have had to shut down email completely for two of my large web sites, because for many years, I failed to protect my email addresses displayed on various pages on my web site (like the *About us* and *Contact us* pages), and thousands of spam bots were able to siphon off these email addresses of my web pages.

These bot owners also sell huge collections of such stolen email addresses disguised as "Double-optin Mailing Lists" to unsuspecting and newbie marketers online. If you've ever seen an offer online or in your email for 10 million email addresses for under $50, then you know what I mean.

So, over a period of time, as my email address got from spammer to spammer, at one point, my BabyNamesIndia.com email addresses were getting about 1000 spam emails *per minute*! It got so bad, that I was kicked out by 3 web hosts, one after the other, all of them refusing to host my web site because of the insanely high volume of emails pouring in every second!

Finally, HostRocket.biz was willing to host my site only as long as I completely turned off my email. So, for many years, I neither promoted nor used any @BabyNamesIndia.com or @CyberConnexions.com email addresses.

But many years later, thanks to Google Apps for Domains (google.com/a), where Google offers an integrated suite of applications like Gmail, Calendar and GooglePages for third-party web sites (like mine), Google now supports my BabyNamesIndia.com email, and because Google is so big and powerful, Gmail is able to take care of all the spam for me. So, I finally have my email back on these domains, and I still see the staggering amount of spam coming in every day in my Gmail-supported spam folders.

But don't let things get to that point where spam becomes a nightmare. Spam is a lot easy to prevent than to fix once it starts pouring in.

Here are a few ways in which you can protect your email addresses on your site.

Use Email Forms

The simplest and most effective way to do it is to remove all references to your email address (no more mailto:Ravi@LinkOverLoad.com text) from your web site, and install a contact-us form on your site.

Anyone who wishes to email you would have to fill out a simple form on your web site – something as simple as entering their name, an email address, subject and the main message – and then using a server-side script like Perl or PHP, you would get the contents of the form emailed to you at a "secret" email address that you have specified in the form-mailer script.

The sender never gets to see your email address; it is not even displayed on your web site. And they really don't need to see it. As long as they are able to send you email, it shouldn't matter to them what your internal email address is, where you will be receiving their email.

Using JavaScript

JavaScript embedded in your HTML page can be used to obfuscate your email addresses so that the web browsers display it correctly at the time of displaying the page to your visitors, but spam-bots that suck email addresses off of web pages, see only gibberish, and text that does not resemble an email address, whereby they are then ignored, thus protecting your email addresses from such bots.

But the downside of this solution is that JavaScript is browser-dependent. Not all browsers render JavaScript the same way, and using a non-reliable technology like JavaScript for a most crucial aspect of your web site – your email address (which is the only way your visitors can get in touch with you) – is probably an unwanted risk that is definitely not recommended.

Using an Image

Using an image that shows your actual email address, which is then linked to the page containing the contact-us form. Even though this is very reliable compared to using JavaScript, this is not a very scalable option, as each time you want to introduce a new email address on your web site, you will have to create a new image, which could turn out to be a hassle.

Email Etiquette

Email is arguably the most powerful communication medium today - because it is cheap, extremely fast, can be personalized, tracked and seamlessly integrated into your web site's marketing strategy.

However, most people don't get it. No, I'm not talking about getting (as in *receiving*) an email sent to you – I'm talking about *understanding* the power of email, and how to use it. In fact, even large companies are clueless about email etiquette and techniques, in spite of having professionals on their payroll worth tens of thousands of dollars who are supposed to be clue-*full*.

Email, as much as it is powerful, can be equally detrimental to the future of both individuals and corporations, if misused or abused. Incorrect and improper email usage can severely impact productivity, adversely affect work quality, waste company resources like bandwidth, cause network congestion, missed project deadlines, upset or put off customers, vendors and affiliates, and even create legal issues.

In this section, you will find many actual examples of both good and bad practices and techniques.

These tips apply to not just emails you send to your customers - but also to those that you send to your friends, colleagues, even your relatives.

DON'T YELL

Do not type using ALL CAPITAL LETTERS. This can be interpreted as YELLING at the person.

Eg: "HOW MANY TIMES DO I HAVE TO ASK YOU BEFORE YOU DO THIS FOR ME?"

Press "CAPS LOCK" to turn capital letters off. Type the email in Caps-and-Lowers.

Don't Exclaim Too Much!!!

Don't use too many ??? or !!! This too means you are yelling at the reader - even if you don't use ALL CAPS.

"I mean, can't you understand even the simplest things????"

"Oh my god, this is ridiculous!!!"

do not use all lower case

Typing without case can be as bad as typing in ALL CAPS. Typing in all lower-case text makes you look unprofessional; or worse, like a newbie (beginner).

And more importantly, people like to see their name spelt correctly (Joe Customer and not joe customer). Typing other people's names in lower case could be seen by some as a sign of disrespect.

"hi joe

please read attached document

ravi"

Make your emails readable

Do not confuse your readers. Use adequate spacing and proper punctuation to clearly communicate your thoughts. Un-clear emails at work often result in the reader replying asking for clarification, usually CC'ing everyone on the list, leading to more junk mail for every one.

Example: "hi ravi sent attached doc"

Does this mean you are saying:

A: "Hi Ravi,

I have sent you an attachment"

- OR -

B: "Hi there,

Ravi sent me the attached document"

Use "CC" and "BCC" wisely

"CC" means "carbon copy". You want to CC person B on an email sent to person A. The email is intended only for A, and you want to send it to B only as a FYI (for your information) about the transaction, and you don't mind A knowing the fact that B is being copied on the email too. For ex., you are sending someone on your team a work request, and you CC your boss so that he is kept "in the loop".

"BCC" means "Blind Carbon Copy". Try to avoid using this altogether, if possible. BCC'ing person B on an email sent to A, means that A does not know that B has been copied on the email, because A does not see B's email address in the "to" list. You should be extremely careful using BCC - because this could lead to many ugly situations. For instance, you could BCC the wrong person on the email, or B, who received the BCC could do a "Reply-All" and the reply would go to A too, and that is when A comes to know that you had BCC'ed B on the email, leading to more ugly situations.

It is better to first send the email to A, and then forward that sent mail from your "sent" folder to person B.

Use "Reply-All" carefully

"Reply All" – the most dangerous button of ‘em all. Believe me when I say that I have actually witnessed a colleague getting fired at work just because they misused it.

Just because someone cc'ed you on an email with 30 others, doesn't mean you should send your reply to all of them. And it also doesn't mean you have the permission to send back an email to every one. You need to use some basic intelligence here to determine whether the email requires you to reply to everyone on the email.

For instance, your boss wants everyone's home address and phone number for his records, to use only during work-related emergencies. He has cc'ed the entire team of 30 people.

Your boss CC'ed the entire team, only because otherwise he would have to send out 30 separate emails with the same request to everyone individually. No one in their right mind would waste 30 minutes doing this.

This does not mean that he wants you to "reply all" and send your reply to all the 31 people on the email. It usually takes one idiot to do this, and then pretty soon everyone else is doing the same, and you come back from your lunch break and see 30 new emails waiting to be read - what a perfect way to waste everyone’s time.

Now consider a different example: A colleague sends out an email to 20 people - and you find that it has incorrect information.

If you replied with the correct information just to the sender, then the sender would then have to forward your email to everyone again, just so that they have the correct information. In this case, you should - and must - do a "Reply All" so that everyone is notified of the correction, and someone else may even have something more to add to your comment.

Another twist to this is if the sender who sent the wrong information is your boss. In that case, you probably don't want to "correct" your boss in public. In which case, you should email her privately about the correction - and it would then give her an opportunity to send out an email himself, correcting the error. And you've then scored yourself some brownie points too.

Cut to the chase

Write concisely. Write to the point. Do not ramble. If someone asks you a question, reply directly to the question. This improves everyone's efficiency and improves productivity.

Include enough detail

While this may seem like a direct contradiction to the above point of cutting to the chase, it actually isn't. Try to include as much detail as necessary in your email, to pre-empt further questions. Incomplete or insufficiently detailed emails can cause repeated inquiries from your customer, and this can be even more frustrating if your customer is in a different time zone and has to wait for at least 24 hours before they can hear back from you.

Satisfying your customers in the first attempt can tremendously reduce refund requests, and will also boost your chances of getting positive word-of-mouth referrals from your customer.

Use personalized, canned emails to speed up repetitive tasks

If you find yourself answering the same questions over and over again, the first thing to do is to put it on a FAQ on your web site and send the sender back a link to the exact FAQ. You can even try to create canned email templates, and copy-and-paste them into your email body without having to type them all over each time.

Also consider using typing automation software, like the one at TypingAssistant.com, which helps you map all of your commonly sent email templates to keywords of your choice, and you can insert long, pre-written, pre-formatted emails in your email body in less than a second, by typing just one word, much like the pop-up helper in Microsoft Word ™.

Attach only relevant files

Don't send large attachments unless they are absolutely required. Especially when dealing with customers, try to publish the file on your web site and send them a link to the file on your site, rather than attaching the entire file in the email itself. Customers can have email accounts with free web mail services like Hotmail or Gmail, or even their own domain-based accounts with even more limited space. You could end up clogging their limited space with your attachment and prevent them from receiving other personal email.

Attachments also cause increased storage requirements, not to mention network congestion at work, thus slowing down every one on your company network.

Use acronyms sparingly

Acronyms like BTW (by the way) and FYI (for your information) can help save a lot of typing time at work when it is between team members or between employees of an organization. But try not to use it with customers, who many not be familiar with their usage, especially if you have customers

Send personalized emails

It is a well-known fact that emails that has the reader's name (preferably first name) in the subject and in the email opening greeting, tends to not only have a higher open rate, but are also more persuasive in their message than their non-personalized counterparts.

Personalized emails also help readers distinguish your emails from other junk mail in their mail box, as spammers are less likely to have your first name, and are even less likely to spell it correctly with the right case.

Do not use the "To" field to list out hundreds of recipients, even if you personally know all of them. Every one on that list will then be able to see everyone else's email address, and that is widely considered a breach of privacy, as the recipient has not given you the permission to broadcast his email address to others. Doing so also opens up people's email address to spammers.

Do not use the "BCC" field to send out bulk mail. Though this is a much better way of emailing a large group than putting them all in the "To" or "CC" field, it still looks very unprofessional, because the recipient sees only one email address in the "To" or "CC" field, and that email address is most probably not theirs. Also, you cannot send personalized emails this way.

Use mail-merge software

Use software like `WebmasterInABox.net/mailmerger.html` to send personalized bulk mail, or if you must use desktop software (not recommended), then use `Post-master.net` or Corey Rudl's `Marketingtips.com/mailloop`.

Never send email in a rage

Sitting in their cubicles, hiding behind the privacy or anonymity of an email address, people tend to write things in an email that they would never have otherwise said to anyone in person. Make it a point to never send out an email when you are highly emotional.

Emotional emails typed in a hurry are probably the most regretted actions in the universe. Emails are perfectly legal documents - equivalent to those that have your signature on them. Anything you write is recorded, and can be, and will be produced in court if necessary, by your employer or Internet service provider.

Don't be fooled into thinking that if it is not on your computer, it is gone forever. Emails have a funny way of turning up at the strangest mail boxes. Copies of emails sometimes can be left on more than one server, as they make their way from their origin to their destination.

Formatting

Write in short paragraphs. Long winding paragraphs are not only hard to read, they are also hard to understand. Traditionally, in email marketing, it is also common to keep the length of each line of your email copy less than 65 characters.

This is because your email doesn't word-wrap, the content stays formatted exactly as you formatted it and not depending on the window size of your recipient's email client, and is easy to read even if your recipient has a low-resolution monitor and is using large fonts.

Use a sample hyphenated line with 65 hyphens (dashes) as a guide when typing your emails. Here's an example:

```
-----------------------------------------------------------------
Make sure all text below is less than the length of the above
dotted line. If you do happen to pass the line as you are
typing, go back to the word that is jutting past the
above line and enter a line break (by pressing "Enter") so
that your email continues on the next line.
-----------------------------------------------------------------
```

Once you finish typing your email, don't forget to delete the guide before you hit the "Send" button.

Better yet, use the free email formatting desktop tool at DesktopDashboard.com which lets you format un-wrapped, long-lined emails to 60 or 65 characters at the click of a button.

Email Signatures

Signatures can be very powerful in conveying a subtle message. It can be used for a "PS" (post script), you can enter your web site url or a marketing message or promotion, or a slogan, or anything to add value to your bottom-line.

Some use it for listing out just their contact info. I personally prefer to list out a special promo going on at that time, or you can even customize the signature specifically to your recipient, and even promote a special offer for that client.

Commercial messages or ads are not allowed on many email and web forums online. In that case, the email signature is a common place to place your promotional messages. This is a generally accepted practice that webmasters and list owners don't mind, as long as the signature is not too long or does not have any offensive or inflammatory content.

Using typing automation software like the TypingAssistant (`VirtualTypingAssistant.com`), you can even frequently rotate your signatures, to generate suspense, intrigue, or curiosity among your readers.

Here are some signatures I use personally:

Ravi Jayagopal
PS: Check out my blog @ http://RavisRants.com

Ravi Jayagopal
Founder & Software Architect
http://WebmasterInABox.net

Ravi Jayagopal
PS: Check out my revolutionary NEW
ClickBank Download Protector Script
http://WebmasterInABox.net/download_protector_clickbank.html

Ravi Jayagopal
Typing On Steroids
http://VirtualTypingAssistant.com

Ravi Jayagopal
Free Affiliate Link Cloaker - and 14 other F`ree Scripts
http://WebmasterInABox.net/alc.html

Ravi Jayagopal
Free Web Site Monitoring Software
http://DesktopDashboard.com

Email Addresses and URL's

Not all email clients have been created equally. Some of them highlight links in the body of the emails such that when your reader moves their mouse over them, the cursor changes to a "hand" thereby making the link "clickable". But then, some don't.

Your best bet is to add the text "http://" to all links in the body of your email. (ex., instead of "Webmasterinabox.net", you way want to type in "http://www.WebmasterInABox.net" - that way, the text appears as an actual link to your recipient).

Email addresses are another type of link to watch out for. You may want to add the text "mailto:" before email addresses that are included specifically in the body of your email, so that they too become "clickable" in case the recipient wants to send you a quick email (other than being able to "reply" to the email, of course).

E.g.,: "Feel free to send me an email at mailto:Ravi@WebmasterInABox.net if you have any questions or concerns".

Using Proper Case in Your Web Site Links

WebmasterInABox.net is clearly more readable than webmasterinabox.net, won't you agree? Try to use caps-and-lowers when typing your web site(s) name(s) so that they are more readable, and thus become more click-worthy.

Escaping Potential Spam Words

In your email body, you may need to break-up words that may match commonly used spam words and trigger spam filters, causing your email to end up in your subscriber's "Junk" or "Spam" folder, or even be deleted permanently by spam filters.

So, instead of the text `free` in your email, you could use ``f`ree`` (notice the subtle apostrophe [single quote]) which will (hopefully) trip up the spam filter, but at the same time will not reduce readability.

24. Web Site Programming

Along the same lines of web site design, you will need some special programming to carry out some special tasks (that HTML and JavaScript are incapable of). Once again, I do not recommend you learn programming, as this is more complex than HTML.

This book is not about teaching you how to become a web site designer or developer. There are a number of great books and resources for that. So, we won't go into any technical details about design or development. But in order for you to get the complete picture, you still need to be aware of all of the components that go into building a web site. So, this chapter is more of an "FYI" than a tutorial.

The components of a web site mentioned in the last chapter, include letting your visitors email right from a contact-us form your web site and not have to use their own email software, or use a web mail service Yahoo mail or Gmail.

You will also need autoresponder software, shopping cart software, visitor tracking software (to see how many visitors your site is getting, where they are coming from, how many pages they visited, etc), advertisement tracking (to see how your online ads are doing), and so on.

Of course, some of the ones just mentioned are for advanced site-owners, and you certainly won't need them all when you are just starting out.

You are also better off using free and open source software, or even purchasing low cost, ready-made scripts that get the job done, which is much cheaper and convenient than learning it yourself, or even hiring someone else to do it for you.

- Contact-Us Form Mailer
- List Management
- Autoresponders
- Forums
- Blogs
- Shopping cart
- Download Protectors
- Password-protected Members-only area
- Affiliate Program Management
- Visitor & Campaign tracking

What I Use

Google Analytics: (Google.com/analytics) For site traffic monitoring

AutoResponse Plus (`AutoResponsePlus.com`): For sequential autoresponders with attachments, newsletter delivery, etc.

WebmasterInABox.net: I have developed my own PHP scripts, some of which are powered by a MySQL database, which I eventually compiled into an off-the-shelf digital product at WebmasterInABox.net

1SiteAutomation.com: For web site automation like shopping cart, affiliate management, autoresponders, bulk emailing and link tracking

For a complete list of what I use and recommend, see the chapter "Ravi Recommends".

25. Your Biggest Challenges

> "This fellow Ford is like a postage stamp. He sticks to one thing until he gets there"
>
> – Thomas Alva Edison about Henry Ford

When Tommy was seven years old, his school teacher labeled him *slow-learner*.

Many years later, as a young man, he repaired the Gold Exchange's telegraphic gold-price indicator and received $40,000 for not only fixing it, but in fact improved the old model.

During one of his experiments, Tommy tried over ten thousand different – and failed each and every single time.

On October 21, 1879, after the 10,001st try finally worked, Tommy, whose full name was "Thomas Alva Edison", showed the world the very first incandescent light bulb.

"I didn't fail ten thousand times. I successfully eliminated, ten thousand times, materials and combinations which wouldn't work", said Edison.

Your biggest challenge in succeeding will not be your idea. It won't be how amazing your product is. It will not be how deep your wallet is, or what car you drive, or what community you live in. It will not matter what language you speak, what God you believe in, what color your skin is.

The only things that matters will be how hard – and smart - you are willing to work.

You may have heard the saying, "Work smart, not hard". Personally, I think that is sheer nonsense.

When you work hard, you become smarter. Yes, that is an absolute given. I am living proof of that.

As a young man, I never put in 100% into anything – not into studies, not into sports. I always did enough to get by.

Many years later, during the time I created WebmasterInABox.net , I realized my true passion was programming – not just for my employer during the day, but for myself, during nights and weekends, and every bit of spare time I could manage.

I have personally experienced my level of intelligence grow exponentially in the last 10 years, just because I was constantly doing a lot of constructive thinking in the form of continuous analysis, problem solving and troubleshooting about various aspects of my e-business.

If I was not thinking about how to make my web sites sell better, I was thinking about what new product to create, how to serve my customers better, how to automate by web site better so that I will be left with more time on the most important task at hand, or about getting more traffic and improving my sites' conversion rate.

You can work both "smart*er*" and "hard*er*".

Darwinism Remix'd

"Survival of the fittest" was Charles Darwin's theory. Boy, am I glad the theory works, on many levels.

I was telling a friend - let's call him Mr. "X" - about Robert Allen, the real estate mogul, who not only made and continues to make millions in real estate, but has trained and mentored average folks like you and me into making millions themselves.

Robert Allen is one of the few geniuses so confident about his strategies, that just to prove that they work, he actually pulled a guy randomly out of the line at the unemployment office, and mentored him to make a deal worth a few hundred thousand dollars, in just a few days.

I'm not saying I recommend buying Robert Allen's courses. I'm just trying to make the point, that if you have initiative, you can always figure out a way to distinguish yourself from the others, and be successful in no matter what you are doing.

I was telling "X" about how real estate was a good venue for making some good money if one were really interested and driven – maybe even enough to quit your day time job some day, and that the fastest way to find out if it is for you is to invest in a few courses which can cut your learning curve and time to a fraction, even if they are a little expensive to begin with.

"X" was hardly impressed - he immediately dismissed the idea of success in real estate by saying, "if it is so easy, then every one would be a millionaire".

"That, my dear "X", is the whole point", I said.

I told him that those who are making tons of money in real estate are lucky to be surrounded by people like "X". If every one took action, and aggressively started going for the same piece of the real estate pie, then the business would no longer be that profitable, would it?

Here's how things get filtered out in life: Of the billions of people in this world…

Only a few dream about being successful.

Of *those* few, only a few ever get off their butt and *want* to do something.

Of *those* few, only a few actually get down to actually *doing* something.

Of *those* few, only a few actually *learn how* to do it right.

Of *those* few, only a few do it with *focus*, without getting distracted.

Of *those* few, only a few *strive* to keep on going, *without quitting* too soon.

Of *those* few, only a few go on to actually *reach the end*, and become successful.

Of *those* few, only a few go on to *maintain* success for life.

Charles Darwin called it "Survival of the FITtest". I call it "Surival of the 'FEW'est"!

Regardless of whether it's Bob Allen's course, or some other Internet guru's course, the few who remain standing at the very end, after life's natural process of elimination, are the ones that manage to achieve their dreams, live their dreams, and be everything they ever wanted to be.

Go on and be everything you've ever wanted to be. No one is stopping you.

No one can ever stop you - except you.

Idle Genius is Worthless

I have another friend – let's call him "Z". Now Z is a great guy, who wants to make a lot of money in life. He wants to be able to afford all the good things in life and have a good time - nothing wrong with that.

But what is he doing about this goal of his? Absolutely Nothing! During one conversation, as I started giving him ideas about what all he could do to achieve his goal, he mentioned that he is not interested in doing any of those things that I just mentioned – and that he would rather just wait for that one "Eureka" moment – when he will get that "Billion Dollar Idea" – sell the idea to some company for royalties or maybe even create and sell the product himself.

Until that day comes around, what was he going to be doing? Believe it or not, he just plans on sitting on his behind doing absolutely N-O-T-H-I-N-G (other than going to work and carrying out all his other family responsibilities, of course).

Edison once said "Genius is 1% inspiration and 99% perspiration". There are two ways to look at it.

You could either sit around goofing off in your spare time, and pray that somehow, miraculously, you will get hit by that "brilliant world-beating idea" (I don't know how though – maybe by watching a lot of science fiction movies?).

Or you could go out there and start doing whatever little you can – take whatever idea you get – run with it.

When you are trying to lose weight, you absolutely have to lose an ounce before you lose a pound – lose a pound before you lose 10 pounds – lose 10 before you can lose a 100.

As you get better at what you do, think more, work harder, expend all your energy, time and effort at being the best at what you do and at doing it better every single day, go through the uphill task of learning, doing, making mistakes, learning from your mistakes, meet different people along the way, learning from their mistakes and successes, then maybe you will have a much greater chance of going somewhere in life.

Don't misunderstand Edison's words.

Don't sit around waiting for that 1% to happen. It won't. It never will. It never does.

Start by putting in the other 99%. Somewhere along the way, you will know when that elusive 1% hits you right in your face.

The Birth of a Product

Initiative opens up doors where there were none before.

When I was dealing with web programming issues for my own web sites, I had a choice: I could have outsourced my programming needs – by either hiring someone, or by purchasing off-the-shelf programming; or since I was a programmer (non-web) by profession, I could learn "web" programming myself, and not only save quite a bit of money, but also add many new skills to my resume – skills that I may not have gotten otherwise.

When I first started working on programming for my own site, the only goal was to learn new technology while saving money working on some cool stuff for my web site.

One day, one of my subscribers emailed me out of the blue and asked me if I could write him a script (a computer program that runs on a web site) similar to one that he had seen on my web site.

And he was willing to pay me for it.

And I thought to myself, "This is a really neat way to make some extra pocket change." I had this program readily available, working and running on my site. All I had to do was copy it over to his site, make a few changes to suit his web site, and he would send me the money. No sweat, right?

He went on to purchase more such scripts from me, and every time he wanted to make some changes to the script settings, he would ask me to do it for him, and it would end up costing him some more.

I realized that if we kept this on, pretty soon not only would I have no time to work on his needs in a timely manner, but he would probably run out of money long before I ran out of time.

The key was to allow him to do it himself – while making it easy enough for a non-techie, non-computer-programmer to install, modify and maintain.

Was that a million dollar idea? You bet it was!

It wasn't a million dollar idea because I was the first to think of it – no way, I was probably 87,345th person to think of customizable, off-the-shelf scripts.

It was a big deal only not all 87,344 people who thought about it before me actually did anything about it – it was a big deal because I followed the idea up with a full blown, professional web site, with multiple such scripts that came with extremely simple instructions to help non-programmers to install such scripts on their own site.

That was the birth of my site WebmasterInABox.net. And I have monthly checks and deposits that predict that I will be reaching my first million dollars in sales sooner rather than later - most of it while I was sleeping , or away at my day job – something I would have never been able to accomplish with just my day job.

Your To-Do List

This is where you "start before you start before you start".

Yes, you can publish a successful web site that sells products or services for hundreds of thousands of dollars a year (or even month), all from your basement, while wearing your pajamas.

But the level of effort, discipline and passion – not to mention certain crucial skills – that are required, are not really that easy.

In this section, I start with some very basic skills which will need to learn, if you don't already have them, and things that you will have to do, in order to make those hundreds of thousands of dollars from your basement, wearing your pajamas.

Learn to Type

As obvious as this seems, you would be surprised to know how many people today work with computers full time, yet poke and prod at the keyboard with two fingers.

No accomplished person became successful without acquiring (if not mastering) some of the basic skills related to their primary profession or career.

Ok, so maybe you have heard of a successful book author who doesn't know typing. But those folks are the exception to the rule (maybe they used speech-recognition software that translates dictated words into text).

But have you heard of an author who did not know the language or know how to write)? Or a basketball pro who didn't work at least a few hours a day to increase his skills, endurance and power? Or a doctor who doesn't know how to use a stethoscope?

Do not base your life or your business on the freaks and exceptions. There's only one person from among tens of millions of people who wins the mega-millions lottery jackpot. Doesn't mean you will too.

How well you do in your e-Business will come down to how much you can get done, and how well you do them. The one basic hurdle you don't want to deal with is your inability to type and wasting hours poking at the keyboard with two index fingers to type even the shortest of emails or updating your web site copy.

If you want to be successful as an e-Business owner and entrepreneur, you will need to know typing, period.

Learn to Write

You will need to polish your communication skills if you want to sell anything at all on your web site.

No, you don't have to have a Shakespearean-vocabulary, or write text that flows like poetry, like my Guru Roy Williams.

However, you will still need a decent level of writing skills – with proper grammar, punctuation, spell-checking et al – to be able to persuade your visitor.

Of course, you can always outsource your writing, but a third-person can never add personality to your web site copy the way you can – because this is your baby – and only you can *feel* your passion.

Trade Recreational Activities for Your E-Business

The very first thing I recommend to any one who wants to be anything in life, is *stop watching TV.*

Yes, TV – that idiot box – that worthless piece of junk in everyone's home which sucks the life, brilliance, ambition, and success out of billions of people worldwide.

Now, I don't mean to sound like your grandmother. I watch TV myself, but only when I really need a break. That too, never for more than a couple of hours a week – most of it over the weekend.

Many years ago, when I was naïve enough to get caught in Multi-Level Marketing (MLM), sophisticatedly labeled as "Network Marketing" - I was trying to convince a prospective sucker that he should buy that brilliant, life altering, herbal medicinal product from me.

This guy had been in MLM before – and he mentioned to me that the main reason he had failed in his previous attempts at MLM, was only because he simply did not have enough time to put in the effort that is needed to take him to the next level (from losing money month after month, to a bare minimum of breaking even, that is).

As I got around to chatting with him, he told me his daily schedule in the evenings – he said he watched TV every single night from 9 PM till midnight. He rattled off names of some "really awesome" shows that he never missed; he went on to say how after that "long, hard day" (of watching stupid TV shows!) he just didn't have the time or energy for anything. And he was not even apologetic about the 3 hours of watching TV! He made it sound like he was genuinely busy doing something important.

My friend "Z" is quite similar. He makes about $40,000 per year. But he drives a $40,000 Lexus. That's one entire year of earnings – actually probably a few years worth of income if you take out the expenses, and add in the interest – that he blew that away on something he really didn't need, and really couldn't afford.

He complains about never having enough time to do anything, yet he watches at least 2 hours of TV every single day, lots more during the weekend, takes afternoon naps during the weekends, and spends away much of his spare time listening to music and thinking about what new DVD or music CD to buy.

Loving What You Do or Doing What You Love?

These are the sacrifices I have had to make in my life in order to get anything done with my web sites.

I could watch TV….	…or I could work on my web site
I could read fiction novels	…or I could read books on technical subjects, marketing and anything that will help me learn skills that can make my e-business better.
I could read magazines when I go to bed…	…or I could read books like the Wizard of Ads Trilogy.
I could read a newspaper in the toilet…	…or I could catch up with technical journals and tech magazines.
I could watch TV….	…or I could work on the next edition of my newsletter
I could relax and listen to music…	…or I could be working on my autoresponder series
I could sleep 8-10 hours a night	Or I could sleep 5-6 hours and use the extra time to spend time with my family, and do the things that have to get done around the house.
I could take an afternoon nap on the weekends	…or I could be working on improving my scripts at WebmasterInABox.net and writing new scripts
I could read entertainment news online during breakfast and lunch at work	…or I could catch up on what my "Drona's" (my involuntary "Guru's") like Seth Godin and Roy Williams are writing in their newsletters, in their blogs, in their articles and on their web sites.

I could sit with a group of friends and yak away for an hour at lunch.	Or I could have a private lunch date with my computer reading different folk's newsletters – many of them from Internet marketers I admire – some of them from my competitors – and sometimes just stuff to update myself with the latest happenings in the Internet world.

Well, maybe I sound like a workaholic after reading about the things I have given up in life. The truth is I'm not.

I only do this because I am doing what I love.

There is "loving what you do". And then there is "doing what you love" (yes, there is a difference between the two).

And then there is "hating what you do".

Hating what you do is when you hate everything about your work (more often than not, this work is your "job"). You hate getting up in the morning, you hate going to work, you hate being there, you hate dealing with people, you hate the people you run into while getting there and coming back, you dread coming back the next day even as you drive back home, and you get depressed at night thinking about next day's work.

And the cycle just goes on. I know it because I have been there. There is no greater hell than having an abusive boss – and worse yet, having a job that you hate.

You will never succeed in life if this is where you are right now. I'm not going to into details about why you have to do what you love. But I do want to say that doing what you love is not the same as loving what you do.

Doing what you love is infinitely more powerful than simply loving what you are already doing.

This subtle difference can be the difference between being above average and being super successful in life.

I was able to give up all those things I mentioned above not just because I wanted to be successful in life and wanted to give myself and my family the best in life.

It helped a lot because I absolutely love working for myself – and I love programming, and working on solutions to problems – and helping others, and making money in the process. So truly, I didn't really feel like I was really "sacrificing" anything.

When I get pulled away from working on my web site to do other chores, I feel like the child who gets pulled away from playing a video game (or some other really fun thing) to do his homework.

It's like the incessant smoker who smokes when he's happy, smokes when he's sad, smokes when he's overworked, smokes when he's bored, smokes on weekdays, smokes on weekends, smokes before going to bed, smokes after getting up – he doesn't even need an excuse to smoke.

When you are addicted to something, you will make up any excuse just to do it.

My work is an addiction for me. My entertainment is working on my site. My relaxation is working on my site. My tranquilizer is working on my site. I work on my site when I'm happy, and I work on it when I'm not. I work on it when I need a break, and I work on it when I'm bored.

You get the idea. You've *got* to find what you really love. And then *do it.*

26. Ideas: Not Worth The Paper They're Written On

Ideas are worth absolutely nothing if they're not followed up with action. Not just any action, but action with a plan to succeed, extraordinary passion, and down-and-dirty execution – day in and day out.

People have "Idea!" moments all the time. Ideas are as common as dirt. Ambition is probably the only thing more common than people with ideas.

Have you ever met anyone who has no ambition in life? Actually, I have - but let's just say that it is not very often that you meet one.

Ambition and ideas are both worthless - without initiative.

"Initiative means you take action. You work with what you've got. You never stand around waiting for instructions. You do something, even if it's wrong", writes Roy Williams, in "The Wizard of Ads – Turning Words into Magic and Dreamers into Millionaires". 'Nuff said.

The Bayonne Bleeder

"He was called the *Bayonne Bleeder* for the punishment he took during his fights.

Chuck Wepner must have felt that the heavyweight championship was his as he saw Muhammad Ali go down as a result of a right hand to the chest. It was not to be as Ali staggered back to his feet and continued to batter the "Bayonne Bleeder" and eventually stopped Wepner with only 19 seconds left in the fight", writes Tom Denelson of Inside Boxing.

Wepner never won a major championship, but did become immortalized in history in a way that no one could ever have imagined.

On that fateful night, as Chuck Wepner came back to take blow after brutal blow from Ali, a young, impressionable and unknown Philadelphia resident was watching on closed circuit TV.

Inspired by Wepner's relentless comebacks, this young man went home that night and wrote the screenplay for what would become not only one of the greatest movies of all time, but also gave birth to arguably the greatest American icon.

The writer of "Rocky" would later go on to become hugely popular in hundreds of countries around the world, as the Italian Stallion.

"Wepner was what one would call 'a catcher", writes Tom, "a fighter who often used his head to block the other guy's punches- not the kind of strategy that leads to long careers. Wepner actually began fighting after he left the Marines at the age of 24 and never truly learned the craft of boxing. At 6'5" and over 220 pounds, Wepner was a giant in his era and his style was plodding and awkward. He constantly pressured his opponent until he either won or was knocked out. He never truly cared how many shots he would absorb before landing the telling blow".

Wepner was offered a choice by Stallone – receive $70,000 upfront, or 1% of the profits of a movie that was not yet made.

Chuck – who had never heard of Stallone - opted for cash upfront in lieu of unseen profits. And he lost over $8,000,000 (yes, 8 Million dollars) as Rocky went on to make over $800 million in profits the world over.

Stallone had an idea after watching Chuck Wepner that night. He could have gone home that night, watched TV, and gone to bed. Instead, he was super-motivated to go beyond 32 previously-rejected scripts to write his 33rd script for the next three days.

Rocky was born because Stallone had initiative. And a movie star was born because a no-name spectator watching from the sidelines, had initiative.

If you read this book, then it means that you already have the initiative. All that remains to be done is to turn your ideas into reality.

When Work Is As Good As Sex...

Doing what you love is like the greatest sex you have ever had - you fantasize about it, you crave for it, you long for it, you wish you could be doing it right now.

If you don't know what makes you tick, it is still worth doing something constructive, rather than sit around watching TV.

When work is as good as sex, you cannot help but achieve super-success.

Good luck and God speed!

27. What Next?

Check out the following web sites for updates and supporting information relevant to the content of this book.

Book's web site: `NBLEB.com`

Bonuses that you got with this book: `NBLEB.com/bonuses.php`

Ravi's Recommendations: `RaviRecommends.com`

Ravi's Blog: `RavisRants.com`

Ravi's Other Web Sites Worth Visiting

LinkOverLoad.com: Web-based Feed Reader (highly customizable) – make this your home page and see the difference.

1SiteAutomation.com: Online, hosted services to automate your e-business

VirtualTypingAssistant.com: Productivity software to speed up your typing

SplashPageGenerator.com: PHP script to automate generation of splash pages

BabyNamesIndia.com: Indian baby names, E-book with 17,347 names

DesktopDashboard.com: Utility software for webmasters and e-business owners

CheapDomains.ws: Domain names so cheap, even your dog will want one.

CheapDomainResellers.com: Start your own domain name registration and hosting service in minutes – completely customizable.

MyCuteCard.com: Send e-greeting cards with your own pictures

HowToThrowYourVoice.com: A site about ventriloquism

WilsonTheWiseOne.com: Ravi's favorite alter-ego, Wilson.

Printed in the United States
125405LV00001B/115/A